Women at the Table

Three Medieval Theologians

Marie Anne Mayeski

A Michael Glazier Book

LITURGICAL PRESS

Collegeville, Minnesota

www.litpress.org

A Michael Glazier Book published by the Liturgical Press

Cover design by Joachim Rhoades, O.S.B. Cover photo courtesy of Corbis Images.

1	2	3	4	5	6	7	8

Library of Congress Cataloging-in-Publication Data

Mayeski, Marie Anne.
    Women at the table : three medieval theologians / Marie Anne Mayeski.
        p.   cm.
    "A Michael Glazier book."
    Includes bibliographical references and index.
    ISBN 0-8146-5829-6 (pbk. : alk. paper)
    1. Christian women saints—Biography—History and criticism.
2. Theology, Doctrinal—History—Middle Ages, 600–1500.   3. Turgot,
d. 1115. Vita Margaritae.   4. Margaret, Queen, consort of Malcolm III, King
of Scotland, ca. 1045–1093.   5. Baudonivia, 6th–7th cent. Vita Radegundis.
6. Radegunda, Queen, consort of Chlotar I, King of the Franks, d. 587.
7. Rudolf, of Fulda, d. 865. Vita Leobae abbatissae Biscofesheimensis.
8. Leoba, Saint, d. 779.   I. Title.

BX4656.M46   2004
274'.03'0922—dc22

                                                    2004004072

To Bill,
in joy and gratitude for
new beginnings.

Contents

Preface

Biography was an important genre for the early Christian theologians. Major theologians such as St. Athanasius of Alexandria and St. Jerome wrote biographies of the desert dwellers and St. Augustine used autobiography to explore the nature of God. For these early masters, writing the lives of the saints was a genuinely theological exercise. In spite of this, medieval hagiography has almost never been accorded careful theological scrutiny. Bring up the topic of medieval theology in a group of theologians, and everyone assumes that the conversation is about Aquinas or his scholastic predecessors. Theological work on the Christian tradition has focused almost exclusively on philosophical treatises and the on-going attempt to retrieve the tradition as it developed in the Middle Ages has virtually ignored the abundant sources in the hagiographical tradition. Such a concentration has forced women's voices to the outermost periphery of theological interest. It has also significantly impoverished our present understanding of the tradition. This study will be a significant move to correct that trend in theological scholarship.

The first chapter will consider the reasons for contemporary theological neglect of hagiographical sources, especially in the light of the scholarship of social historians who find them both rich and persuasive. It will also consider the evidence that justifies a theological reading for hagiographical texts. This evidence includes the explicit intentions that medieval hagiographers give for their writing and their descriptions of its character. Finally, the first chapter will also suggest the methodological issues that govern a retrieval of the narrative sources.

Three case studies follow by way of example. The first in a theological analysis of Rudolf of Mainz's life of St. Leoba in the context of the ninth-century Carolingian Empire. St. Leoba was an Anglo-Saxon missionary to Germany; her life exposes significant ecclesiological themes as well as related presentations of Christology and anthropology. The second case study focuses on the life of Margaret, Queen of Scotland, written in the very early twelfth century for her daughter, newly crowned queen of Norman England. In this study the major themes cluster around the issues of inheritance and genealogy, with questions about original sin, inherited virtue, and the redemptive character of childbearing. In the final study, the text is Baudonivia's life of Radegunde, a queen of sixth-century Francia. This life is an exposition of a theology of power, as understood by those usually excluded from it, in the light of the cross of Christ.

I have chosen these three texts because, first, they were written closely in time to the saint's actual life and contemporary sources, written or oral, are identified in all three texts. This awareness of historicity by the original authors, even when their norms of what is historical differ significantly from our own, indicates their understanding of the importance of history in Christian theology. Second, they were all written during periods of noteworthy theological transition, when external circumstances required noteworthy adaptations of church tradition. The Christian tradition is an organic reality whose developments are always in response to the external stimuli of new contexts, new pastoral needs, and new cultural values. A new context means that institutions and beliefs that have been assumed and accepted become once again the matter for discussion.

Finally, I have chosen these texts because women played a part in their creation as well as being their subjects. Baudonivia, the author of the life of Radegunde, is one of the few named women authors in the early Middle Ages and, as such, deserves a very careful reading. Rudolf acknowledges and names the women whom he uses as sources for his text. They were women who knew St. Leoba personally. In the case of the life of St. Margaret, her daughter commissioned the text, and there is significant textual evidence that the author, a monk who served as St. Margaret's chaplain, has her daughter in mind, particularly when crafting his descriptions of Margaret's virtues.

The connection of these texts with the lives and world of women is important to this study. In these texts women play some part in the theological conversation that created them and subsequently arose around them. In *Writing a Woman's Life,* a feminist analysis of women's biographical writing, Carolyn Heilbrun gives a clear and helpful definition of power: "[It] is the ability to take one's place in whatever discourse is essential to action and the right to have one's part matter."[1] Among the many ways in which women have been denied power within the Christian Church has been their routine and consistent exclusion from the theological conversation. Denied ordination to significant places in ministry and habitually denied the education that would have enabled them to have significant influence, women could and did act on behalf of the Church. They could become holy and esteemed and create institutions within which churchmen could exercise their influence, but they could not enter easily into the theological discourse that shaped their lives and their faith. Their lives, however, were recorded in large numbers and if we understand that the texts that lauded their accomplishments were genuinely theological texts, then, through them and in them, they were "at the table" where theological conversations took place. In that sense, the women of these texts, whether they play the role of subjects, sources, author or intended audience, exercised some theological power in their formulation. They helped to shape the theology that is exposed in the texts, a theology that, although it is not exclusively about them, includes them in its discussion of central issues of the tradition.

---

[1] Carolyn Heilbrun, *Writing a Woman's Life* (New York: Ballantine Books, 1988) 18.

Acknowledgments

The author gratefully acknowledges the assistance and support of generous colleagues, several of whom read sections of this work when it was in progress. Fr. James Fredericks, Ph.D., Sr. Mary Beth Ingham, Ph.D., Dr. Lizette Larson-Miller, and Fr. Thomas P. Rausch, Ph.D., gave helpful criticism along the way, although the final work and its conclusions remain my own responsibility. Dr. Jane Crawford and Fr. William Fulco, Ph.D., brought their Latin expertise to bear on my reading of the original medieval texts. I am also grateful to Loyola Marymount University whose generous Summer Research Grant permitted me to pursue research for this project in 2000 and 2002.

Sections of this work have appeared previously, for which I thank the various publishers for permission to reprint here. Part of chapter 1 and the ecclesiology in Rudolf's life of Leoba were published in "New Voices in the Tradition: Medieval Hagiography Revisited," *TS* 63,4 (December 2002) 690–710. The analysis of Ælred's thought on natural virtue first appeared in "'Secundam Naturam': The Inheritance of Virtue in Ælred's *Genealogy of the English Kings*," *Cistercian Studies Quarterly* 37.3 (2002) 221–28. I have also previously analyzed Baudonivia's life of St. Radegunde in "Reclaiming an Ancient Story," which is reprinted by permission from *Women Saints in World Religions*, edited by Arvind Sharma, the State University of New York Press © 2000, State University of New York. All rights reserved.

Abbreviations

AASS	*Acta Sanctorum*. Ed., Joannes Bollandus et al. Paris, 1863–
MGH	Monumenta germaniae historica. Hanover, 1823–
	AA: Auctores antiquissimi
	SS: Scriptores
	SSRM: Scriptores rerum merovingicarum
PL	Patrologiae cursus completus, series latina. Ed., J.-P. Migne. Paris, 1844–64
SC	Sources Chrétiennes. Paris, 1943–present
TS	Theological Studies

1

Theology and Narrative Sources: An Introduction

The Current Theological Neglect of the Lives of the Saints

In their investigation of the medieval period of the tradition, Catholic theologians have long privileged the scholastic texts and thinkers. There are many possible reasons for this privilege. The monumental accomplishment of the great scholastics such as Bonaventure and Aquinas has understandably drawn all eyes to their work and tends to dwarf other contributions. Leo XIII's virtual anointing of Aquinas as the normative Catholic theologian in *Aeterni Patris* (1879) only reinforced the implicit consensus that Thomistic theology *is* the medieval tradition. Since Catholic theology after the Reformation retained, and indeed emphasized, its concern for the integration of theology and philosophy, it is logical that contemporary theologians would look to the philosophical sources of the Middle Ages and these, undeniably, are richest during the scholastic period.

But the theologian concerned to understand and build upon the fullness of the Catholic tradition must wonder whether the privileged position of scholastic writers might indeed have blinded us to the theological importance of other texts. To be more specific, one may question whether or not narrative sources, specifically the lives of the saints, have been ignored for the wrong reasons and to the detriment of the Catholic

1

theological project. It is the question of medieval theological sources that this book will address.

To answer this question we must first consider some of the reasons that theologians ignore hagiographical texts. Then we must consider what medieval writers themselves might have thought they were doing when they composed such lives. That will enable us to look, finally, at some particular texts and attempt to give them a theological reading.

Possible Reasons for Ignoring the Lives of the Saints

Certain assumptions made about hagiographical texts contribute to their theological neglect. They are assumed to reflect only "popular religiosity" and, although this makes them valuable in documenting the religious and moral catechesis of the people of God in a variety of contexts, they are usually dismissed as "uncritical" and unrelated to the actual formulation of the tradition itself. The label of "popular religion" does, often rightly, identify the political motives of those who crafted the narrative texts; some are the work of those who sought to elevate the importance (and lucrative potential) of particular shrines or who hoped to control the behavior of the laity by giving them appropriate models of conduct. Such judgments have often been made, however, without careful attention to the provenance of each specific text and this failure is, in itself, seriously uncritical. Without doubt the theological value of these texts is uneven, but, again, the value of each can only be determined by careful study.

Another assumption about medieval narrative texts is that they may be of interest to the field of history, but are problematic for the study of systematic theologians. Certainly historians have found in them rich evidence to document specific lives and communities, evidence that is particularly helpful in illuminating the lives of "the people," ordinary Christians otherwise unnoticed. In a helpful essay entitled "Saints, Scholars and Society: The Elusive Goal," Patrick Geary[1] has identified recent trends in the historical analysis of the *vitae sanctorum*. He notes how historians have discovered the importance of such texts, not only

---

[1] *Saints: Studies in Hagiography,* ed. Sandro Sticca (Binghamton, N.Y.: Medieval & Renaissance Texts and Studies, 1996) 1–22.

for what he calls "incidental historical information" (p. 5), but also for the study of social values.

The importance of hagiographical texts in social history and their strength, particularly, in documenting otherwise neglected lives have brought them to the attention of feminist historians. Scholars like Jane Tibbetts Schulenburg have discovered that, "unlike many other sources of the Middle Ages, saints' lives focus a great deal of attention on women: the *vitae* are directly concerned with female roles in the church and society as well as contemporary perceptions, ideals, and valuations of women."[2] That the ideal of holiness proffered by the *vitae sanctae* was also shaped by gender concerns has not gone unnoticed. Jo Ann McNamara has, for instance, uncovered the textual tradition dependent upon the life of Helena, mother of Constantine. McNamara demonstrates that a feminization—and limitation—of royal power was strongly encouraged by a series of royal women's lives.[3] Similarly, Lois L. Huneycutt has studied how the biblical story of Esther was used to empower medieval Christian queens in their ambiguous position as intercessors with the king.[4]

In all of these fine studies—and many others like them—the specifically religious element of the *vitae sanctorum* has been utilized in three specific ways. One, the Christian values and virtues proposed by the text are understood to reveal the social and religious mores of a given Christian society. Two, the concrete historical details identifiable in the text have been used as windows into the religious activity of persons otherwise undocumented: ordinary Christians and, especially, women of all classes. Three, the religious ideology of Christian faith has been seen in the texts as empowering women and other marginalized groups to act beyond the usual social boundaries of their class and gender. But while the specifically religious content of hagiographical texts does reveal

---

[2] "Saints Lives as a Source for the History of Women, 500–1100," *Medieval Women and the Sources of Medieval History,* ed. Joel T. Rosenthal (Athens and London: The University of Georgia Press, 1990) 285–320.

[3] "Imitatio Helenae: Sainthood as an Attribute of Queenship," in Sticca, *Saints,* 51–80.

[4] "Intercession and the High Medieval Queen: The Esther Topos," *Power of the Weak: Studies on Medieval Women,* ed. Jennifer Carpenter and Sally-Beth MacLean (Urbana and Chicago: University of Illinois Press, 1995) 126–46.

themes and conditions important to Christian history, it does not ensure that hagiographical texts will bear the weight of interest by systematic theologians, even those who seek to understand the full richness
and extent of the Christian tradition.

The very notion of "*the* Christian tradition," however, is itself critically problematic. While the diversity of practice and the presence of
doctrinal debates during the first Christian centuries is widely acknowledged, there often exists an unquestioned assumption that all of the
components of faith and practice that we presently accept as normative
were well in place by the end of the patristic period. To be sure, the
formulation of the creed, the *symbolum fidei,* by the great ecumenical
councils of the fourth and fifth centuries assured the permanence and
orthodoxy of the major creedal formulas. But debate and discussion
continued for centuries and sacramental practice, for instance, continued to retain significant regional differences and to develop along different lines, sometimes parallel, sometimes complementary, often enough
divergent. For much of our history, local theologies continued to exist
within the broad spectrum of orthodoxy permitted by the normative
affirmations of faith found in the creeds.

In his work on Celtic theology, Thomas O'Loughlin has developed
the notion of "local theology" in ways that are helpful to this present
study and, indeed, for all those who would understand the complexity
of the Christian tradition.[5] O'Loughlin points out that, in spite of its
name, a local theology does not necessarily require that those who share
its suppositions and positions be geographically or even temporally
proximate. He posits that a local theology comes from shared cultural
experiences and similar pastoral challenges. He then describes the theology of early medieval Europe as "a patchwork of local theologies that
influence each other for good or ill." He concludes that to reduce the
theological positions of the Frankish monasteries, Visigoth Spain, and
Bede, *inter alia,* to "merely one 'western' [or] 'Latin Catholicism' blinds
us to the rich diversity of [their] texture." Equally, to consider that any
one of these is an aberration from the orthodox tradition is to ignore

---

[5] *Celtic Theology: Humanity World, and God in Early Irish Writings* (London and
New York: Continuum, 2000).

"their own perception of their unity in Christ"[6] and the respect shown to each of them by the larger church.

This understanding of local theology is a more critically credible hermeneutic for understanding the Christian tradition and grasping its complex history. If, then, the Christian tradition can be seen as composed of a variety of local theologies, then to understand it we must consider a wider variety of texts than is presently the case and historical, social and pastoral context is at least as important as genre in grasping the whole picture. Seen from this perspective, hagiographical texts may well assume a central importance.

Getting Inside the Mind of the Authors

To demonstrate that hagiographical narratives can bear the weight of systematic theological investigation, we must attempt to understand how the medieval authors of hagiographical texts viewed their own work. To understand how early medieval theologians might understand and value narrative genres, we must first reflect on the linguistic influences that shaped their thought and writing. They wrote, of course, in a second language, that is, they did not do theology in the language that was the ordinary vehicle of expression in daily life. They learned their theological language almost entirely through the Bible itself. Though many of them had access to certain texts of the classical grammarians, they learned their alphabet from the alphabetic psalms, their grammar from the sentence structures of the Vulgate and their rhetoric from samples culled from the biblical corpus. The *De Arte Metrica* and his *De Schematibus et Tropis* of Bede, an eighth-century Anglo-Saxon monk, are but two examples of the medieval tools that were accessible. This means not only that would they have done theology entirely within the thought-world of the Bible, but that they would have had a high regard for the genres through which divine revelation unfolded. Given the importance of the narrative (or historical) books of the Bible, and especially the privileged position of the Gospels, early medieval writers would certainly have appreciated the theological nature of the narrative form.

[6] O'Loughlin, 23.

Second, we must understand how thoroughly early medieval theologians venerated the work of the Fathers and sought to continue it. In terms of literary genre, the patristic legacy of theological writing was significantly diverse. The great theologians of the first four centuries left many exegetical texts, both commentaries and homilies, as well as treatises that were somewhat more philosophical in nature, such as Tertullian's *De Testimonio Animae* or the *De Trinitate* of Augustine. They also authored important narrative texts that were no less theological than their exegetical work or treatises. Besides disseminating the ideals of asceticism and monasticism, for instance, Athanasius of Alexandria used the Life of St. Antony of Egypt to promote his christological opinions in the murky maelstrom of conflict on the eve of the Council of Nicea. Sulpicius Severus, in his Life of St. Martin of Tours, offers to Christians in the Merovingian kingdom not just the biography of an extraordinary hero, but also a theology of the episcopacy with all of its ecclesiological ramifications. Even as the structures of church governance, crafted within the cultural ideals of the late Roman world, were being extended to peoples with other indigenous traditions (c. 400), Severus tells the story of a Roman soldier who becomes an effective, even forceful, bishop of the Gallic city of Tours. The way in which he makes that personal transition and subsequently leads his city in fidelity to the Gospel becomes an exposition of the possibilities of clerical life and leadership in a missionary context.

No one reading Augustine's *Confessions* can think that it is only his autobiography.[7] Augustine studies the unfolding of his own life because it is the drama of encounter between God and the human person. "Why do you mean so much to me," Augustine asks God early in the first book and then, a few sentences later, he continues to wonder, "and why do I mean so much to you?" The answers to these questions are to be found only in the nature of God and in the created nature of the human person. Thus, Augustine's "autobiography" is at once a biographical narrative and a study of God and of Christian anthropology. Perhaps because

---

[7] Although a review of Garry Wills' book on Augustine's *Confessions* in the *Los Angeles Times* (July 3, 1999) did seem to suggest that Wills was breaking new ground in proposing that Augustine's work was theological rather than pornographic!

the Gospels, which follow a biographical pattern, were accepted as the Church's primary instruments of revelation, biographical texts themselves were essentially theological documents in the first five centuries and this patristic precedent would have weighed heavily with early medieval writers. Gregory of Tours and the Anglo-Saxon Bede extended that tradition into their own historical and cultural milieus in the sixth and eighth centuries. Certainly they used the historical narratives of their respective peoples, including the biographies of individuals, to develop their theologies of Church and sacraments, of history, of kingship, and of the realities of the heavenly kingdom.

We have solid evidence to suppose, then, that the medieval authors of saints' lives understood their narratives as fully theological works; they would, quite simply, not understand our contemporary distinction between hagiography and theology. Two early texts confirm this supposition; they suggest a conscious effort by authors of medieval saints' lives to give their narratives the theological weight of the Gospels and of the work of the Fathers.

The first text is that of Jonas of Bobbio, the preface (chapter 1) to his life of St. Columbanus. Columbanus was the late-sixth-century pilgrim monk from Ireland who founded the important monasteries of Luxeuil and Bobbio. Shortly after his death in 615, Jonas published his *vita* (643) and, in the prologue, the latter carefully lists a kind of canon of saintly biographies, in imitation of which he has penned his own narrative.

> By their shining skill that vibrates with an exceptional brightness, renowned teachers composed the lives of those holy monks and fathers who leaped ahead of the others [in the journey of life] so that the sustaining example of the ancients might pervade the future like perfume. The eternal sower set this in motion from the beginning of all things so that he might make provision for the enduring reputation of his servants. He provided that past deeds would leave behind models for the future, so that [the servants of God] might boast in generations to come, either by imitating the example of those who preceded them or by committing them to memory.[8]

---

[8] Rutilans atque eximio fulgore micans sanctorum praesulum atque monachorum doctrina, Patrumque solertia, nobilium virorum condidit Vitas doctorum, scilicet ut posteri alma redolerent priscorum exempla. Egit hoc a saeculis rerum

Jonas then goes on to list the works that he considers to be covered by this description: Athanasius' life of Antony, Jerome's lives of Paul, the hermit, and Hilary, the three lives of St. Martin of Tours, and the lives of the great bishops Hilary of Poitiers, Ambrose and Augustine (written by Fortunatus, Paulinus and Possidius, respectively). He completes the preface with the usual disclaimer that he has neither the personal holiness nor the skill of the preceding authors, but he also affirms that he is following in their footsteps. We are justified, therefore, in applying his description of patristic biographies to his own work. Whatever it was that the early authors were doing, Jonas of Bobbio intends to do the same.

In the two sentences cited, we note, first, that the work of writing these *vitae* is attributed to God's initiative; they are part of God's providential care of those who become members of the divine household. Second, these *vitae* are intended not just as moral guides ("by imitating their example"), but also are to be "committed to memory." The phrase evokes the importance of *memoria* in the theology and anthropology of the early Middle Ages, especially in monastic contexts. It relates the lives of the saints to the reading of the Word at eucharistic liturgies as well as to the *imago Dei* anthropology in which memory, like the first person of the Trinity, is the source of all that the human person will know, choose and become. Clearly these texts are formative as well as informative, theological as well as motivational.

The second text to consider is that of Rudolf of Saxony. Rudolf was the star pupil of Rabanus Maurus who, in the ninth century, was elevated from being the abbot of Fulda (where he had taught Rudolf) to the episcopal see of Mainz. In an author's preface to his life of Rabanus, Rudolf clearly presents the written narratives of saints' lives as a theological genre, similar to the Scripture and, indeed, a continuation of them.

> The writers of ecclesiastical matters have resolved not only wisely but also usefully and according to the divine precepts to hand over to posterity the lives and deeds of the just through the revelations of litera-

---

Sator aeternus, ut suorum famulorum famam commendaret perennem, ut relinqueret futuris saeculis de praecedentium meritis, vel [**Col. 1014A**] imitanda exempla vel memoriae commendanda, et ut ventura soboles gloriaretur de praecedentium meritis. *PL* 87,1013d-1014A.

ture. Deservedly [these authors] must be extolled by the faithful with great praises because they have not enviously passed over these things in silence. Rather, overflowing with a charity that desires to benefit everybody, they published them, wishing them to be an example of living rightly, imitated by all those faithful who wish to rely on the truth of faith. For if they had not done so, we would not be able to know at all what the holy patriarchs, prophets, apostles, as well as the rest of the holy martyrs and confessors of Christ, had done or taught. Nor would we know by what signs and acts of power they became famous (either before or after their death), except for the things understood and believed from their writings. The authors have revealed these things, not to receive praise for themselves but that through such examples they might incite everyone possible to reform their customary behavior, depraved through human presumption, and to praise greatly the power of the divine majesty.[9]

Then, like Jonas, Rudolf asserts that he is writing to continue this laudable tradition, even while disclaiming his talents. Rudolf's careful use of language here, as well as his rhetoric and the line of his argument, require close scrutiny,

First, we may note that these narratives have been written by those concerned for "ecclesiastical matters," that is, the authors of religious narratives are people of the Church who concern themselves with the full range of church interests—theological, institutional, and pastoral.

---

[9] Scriptores rerum ecclesiasticarum cum sapienter, tum etiam utiliter instituerunt, vitas et facta justorum, et secundum divina praecepta viventium virorum, per litterarum revelationes tradere posteris. Merito a fidelibus magnis ideo laudibus extollendi, quod non invidiose silentes ea praetermiserunt; sed charitate, quae omnibus prodesse desiderat, abundantes, ad exemplum recte vivendi cunctis imitari volentibus fidei veritate subnixi protulerunt. Si enim non ita fecissent, nequaquam scire potuissemus quid sancti patriarchae, quid prophetae, quid apostoli, quid etiam caeteri sancti martyres et confessores Christi gesserint, vel docuerint, quibusque signis et virtutibus ante vel post mortem suam claruerint; nisi ex eorum scriptis credita et intellecta nosceremus; qui ea non captandae propriae laudis intentione protulerunt, sed ut per ejusmodi exempla ad emendandos pravos mores humanae praesumptionis, et ad collaudandam divinae majestatis potentiam quorumcunque animos incitarent. *PL* 107, 41AB. The translation is that of Dr. Jane Crawford of the department of classics and archeology at Loyola Marymount University.

That is also implied by the two adverbs, "wisely" and "usefully," the first of which was commonly applied to theology ("divine wisdom") and the second to pastoral concerns ("useful for Christians"). When Rudolf itemizes the various important narratives in the Christian tradition, he begins with the stories of "the holy patriarchs and prophets" and continues through to include the stories of "the apostles . . . [and] the rest of the holy martyrs and confessors of Christ." Clearly, for Rudolf, the written lives of the saints as he knows them continue the history of salvation begun in scripture. Saints' lives are, in fact, revelatory in a way both similar and comparable to the revelation in the biblical texts.

In describing these texts, Rudolf uses precise theological language: he calls the events narrated the *facta justorum,* that is, the deeds of those who have been justified by divine grace. He uses the technical word *tradere,* or "to hand over," to denote the process by which the author communicates the story; this is the word that, in the vulgate translation of 1 Corinthians 11 Paul uses for the transmission of the institution narrative and in chapter 15 for the similar transmission of the post-resurrection appearance narratives. Thus, Rudolf links his own narrative of Maurus' life all that "tradition" implied for both doctrine and liturgy. And the content of the stories is identified as *revelationes,* the same word, of course, that is used to describe the fullness of the apostolic patrimony. Rudolf further defines the content of these lives—both biblical and later lives—as *credita* and *intellecta;* they teach what is to be believed and what is to be understood. He thus acknowledges that one of the purposes in reading the *vitae sanctorum* is the imitation of the saint's example, but he specifies quite clearly that they also are "to be imitated by all those faithful [who] wish to rely on *the truth of faith*" (emphasis mine). The suggestion is that imitation of good deeds depends upon believing rightly and that these narratives contain not only models of holiness but the truth of doctrine.

Finally, Rudoph notes that the early authors of Scripture and the lives of the saints "hand over [their stories] to posterity . . . through the revelations of literature." This reminds the reader of the discipline of study by which the Christian learned to read biblical texts, with the skills of literary criticism embodied in grammar, logic and, especially, rhetoric. Rudolf clearly believes that the disciplines of biblical interpretation, in which he had been schooled by Rabanus Maurus, must also be applied to the lives of the saints, including those he himself wrote. In sum, these lives of the saints are written by those concerned for ecclesiastical life, they are extensions of the revelatory narratives of Scripture and they contain genuine doctrine that must be both believed in faith and understood by theological reflection and mimetic action. It seems that, in the light of all of the above, there is sound basis for reading the lives of the saints through the lens of doctrinal theology.

Methodological Considerations

A specific methodology structures the theological reading of these hagiographical texts, a method that borrows significantly from the historical critical method of biblical exegetes. First, the texts are analyzed in terms of the social, historical, and cultural context in which they were written. To the degree possible and desirable, the historical situations of both subject and author have been exposed. We consider the political forces at work in the world of the text, as well as the social class and situation of subject, author and audience. Gender issues are necessarily a part of the cultural context and this requires that feminist criticism must be brought to bear on the text. All of this marks an intent to ground the text very specifically in its own time and place, to ground it, as it were, horizontally.

Second, since we presume that the authors intended the texts to be read theologically, they must be placed within the Christian tradition, as it had developed prior to the text. No medieval author wished to compose "new theology"; each considered the theological task to be one that built on Scripture as interpreted by the great theologians that had gone before. Where pertinent, therefore, there will be a consideration of ways in which previous theologians, especially the great Latin Fathers, had considered the themes the author is using. This is an attempt to ground the text vertically, within the ancient and developing tradition.

Third, there will be a close, careful reading of the original text, with attention to specific words and phrases and their theological weight. Translations will be cited in the body of the text, but the original Latin sources will be available in the footnotes, so that the critical reader may investigate the language independently. Finally, the theological themes within the texts will be synthesized and their importance attended to, in some cases using contemporary theological reflection on the themes under consideration.

2

Life of St. Margaret of Scotland by Her Chaplain: A Theology of Inherited Virtue and the Redemption of Childbirth

Inheritance and Genealogy at the Court of Henry I

During the early part of the twelfth century, the Anglo-Norman court of Henry I was the site of a lively conversation about the many dimensions of heredity. Documents reveal a variety of concerns about the legal, social and, even, theological ramifications of inheritance. There were narratives about Henry's own acquisition of the throne; there were legal treatises on tenure and rights. Charters were enacted that affirmed inherited titles and property. Genealogies expanded and became more than simple statements of legitimate birth or symbolic statements of praiseworthy ancestry. This social and political interest provides the context for several explicitly theological developments; it allows the theological reader to understand sections of a Life of St. Margaret of Scotland, written at the beginning of Henry's reign, as an exploration of the possibility that virtue may be part of the legacy of one's ancestors. It also raises the possibility that Anselm of Canterbury's treatise on the Immaculate Conception and original sin can be read, at least in part, as an exposition of inheritance as a theological category.

The world of the text is extremely well documented. Henry I was called, even in his lifetime, the "Beauclerc," a reference to his passion for literary and documentary activity and he initiated/extended the royal chancery where copies of all the texts and monetary accounts produced in the court were kept. We have at least four chronicles or narratives that convey that world from a variety of perspectives. Eadmer, Anselm's friend and biographer contributed *A History of Recent Events in England.*[1] William of Malmesbury, also a Benedictine, was the author of *Chronicle of the Kings of England,*[2] the *Recent History* and the *History of the Bishops of England.* One extant version of *The Anglo-Saxon Chronicle,*[3] probably begun in the late ninth century, covers events up to the middle of the twelfth century and, thus, has entries that document events involving Henry's court. Finally, we have the detailed, comprehensive work of Orderic Vitalis, whose *Ecclesiastical History*[4] remains an indispensable source for Anglo-Norman society. Given all this textual evidence, we are able not only to illumine the forces that shaped the text of St. Margaret's life but to ask the questions that will allow us, I hope, to understand how its themes fit into larger movements and conversations.

Social and Political Documents

During the late eleventh and early twelfth centuries, the Anglo-Norman world was in significant transition from a strict feudal social system to one marked by primogeniture and hereditary rights. The feudal system was theoretically based on the concept that the overlord possessed the land; magnates and other important people received it as a benefice from the overlord, in exchange for various services, chief of which was the knightly obligation to fight on the lord's behalf. Family inheritance had long since replaced the continuing sequence of benefices that returned to the lord on the death of the recipient but, at this moment in Norman England, family inheritance was becoming more and more

---

[1] Trans. G. Bosanquet (London: Cressit Press, 1964).

[2] Trans. J. A. Giles (London: George Bell and Sons, 1895).

[3] Trans. and ed. M. J. Swanton (New York: Routledge, 1998).

[4] Ed. and trans. Majorie Chibnall, in 6 volumes (Oxford: Clarendon Press, 1969–1980).

commonly the inheritance of the first-born. This had consequences all the way to the court. It was, according to M. Chibnall, an eminent scholar of the period, a period of significant transition. "Before the end of the eleventh century the question of how to assess the obligations of vassalage in terms of cash was beginning to make itself felt. Enfeoffments of both tenants-in-chief and a rising number of their knights, and the movements of custom from more general family inheritance of land towards primogeniture inheritance of fiefs, brought about a change in the nature of vassalage."[5]

Narratives of Henry I's seizure of the throne of England document the transitional character of custom and law at the time. William Rufus, son of William the Conqueror, had negotiated for the throne and ruled England as his father willed him to, even though there was an older son, Robert of Normandy (out of favor because his father thought him a traitor). When Rufus died suddenly in a hunting accident in 1100, the next in line, according to primogeniture would have been that same Robert. It would seem that at Rufus' death the nobles of England anticipated some kind of internecine struggle and were not yet confident that their property and titles would remain theirs by hereditary right, but depend rather upon the gift of the king.

Orderic Vitalis in his *Ecclesiastical History* records the dramatic events that followed quickly on the death of William Rufus: "many nobles made off from the wood [where they had been hunting with William Rufus] to their estates and prepared to resist the disorders they anticipated."[6] That is to say, they anticipated the need to defend by force their rights to the estates on which their power and titles depended. Henry himself "galloped at full speed to Winchester castle where the royal treasure was."[7] He wanted to secure the contents of the treasury as evidence of

---

[5] Margaret Chibnall, *Anglo-Norman England 1066–1166* (Oxford: Basil Blackwell, 1986) 116. Chibnall also notes that such a change, from a world where kinship and lordship had equal importance to one in which the importance of lordship dominated, would affect many social situations, including the importance of women pp. 162–63. This makes our text's concentration upon women even more important.

[6] Orderic Vitalis, bk. X, ch. iv, l. 89.

[7] Ibid., X, iv, 88.

his right to inherit and as a source of power to substantiate that right. He was challenged at the gate by one of Duke Robert's men, and showed himself ready to defend his right, not by legal process but by his sword. The struggle betrays all the dynamics of the feudal system. Later on, however, Henry would defend his right to the crown theoretically, by stating that he was the first-born after his father had become King of England through conquest. This is an argument through force of primogeniture. In all actuality, he was in the right place at the right time, born into the right family and quick of wit.

Henry moved to solidify his position by the issuance of the Coronation Charter (August 5, 1100), in which he inaugurates or ratifies rights and privileges important to the aristocracy and to the Church. Among these are the rights of inheritance. Item 1 in the charter contains Henry's promise not to dispossess the Church of any property. Item 2 provides that on the death of a property holder, the heir shall enter into possession of it with a simple payment of money that in no way jeopardized the right of legitimate succession. Henry further notes that this was not the practice "in the time of my brother."[8]

The issues, however, remained alive and a cause for concern. Magnates of England and Normandy met early in Henry I's reign to affirm, *inter alia,* that their ancestors had won their lands by valor and force of arms and that they themselves "honorably enjoyed [those same lands] by right of inheritance under the great dukes up to now."[9] And Henry felt compelled to repeat his promise somewhat later in his reign and in another duchy. Orderic Vitalis, records the incident. "In the middle of October the king came to Lisieux, summoned all the magnates of Normandy and held a council of great benefit to the Church of God. He therefore decreed . . . that all lawful heirs should likewise hold their inheritances."[10] Clearly, throughout the reign of Henry I, the issues of inheritance and primogeniture remained a matter of lively conversation and crucial social importance.

---

[8] *English Historical Documents,* vol. II: 1042–1189, ed. David C. Douglas and George W. Greenaway (London and N.Y.: Oxford University Press, 1981) 433 and 445.

[9] Orderic Vitalis VIII, iii, 269.

[10] Ibid., XI, iv, 234.

It is in this context that we best understand the marriage of Henry to Matilda, daughter of Margaret, the former queen of Scotland and sister of its present king. We have no evidence to suggest that Henry did not love and respect Matilda for herself; in fact, the many chroniclers affirm otherwise. But a royal wedding is always a matter for policy as well as affection and Henry's choice would not have ignored Matilda's royal blood. Through her mother, St. Margaret of Scotland, Matilda was heir both to Anglo-Saxon royalty and to Norman aristocracy. Her ancestry, though not strictly speaking a matter of primogeniture, significantly bolstered Henry's hereditary claim. Orderic Vitalis notes the importance of her royal pedigree (bk. X, iv, 97) but insists that Henry was drawn to Matilda's reputation "for her virtue and holy life" because he himself was wise (VIII, iii, 272).

The Theological Conversation: The Life of St. Margaret

Shortly after she became queen of England, Matilda, daughter of Queen Margaret of Scotland, requested from Turgot, her deceased mother's chaplain,[11] that he write an account of her mother's life and death. In his prologue, Turgot writes of Matilda's "wish to hear" of this holy woman whom she had hardly known in life; her wish accorded perfectly with Turgot's "desire to write" of the dead queen.[12] He had greatly admired Margaret, but, most of all, she had charged him on her deathbed to advise and correct her children, especially those who themselves ascended to royal power. Matilda's request for a written life of her mother gave Turgot a unique opportunity to write a text that would be informative, surely, but formative as well and gave Turgot the occasion to advise the new queen about her royal duties as a Christian queen. The timing was perfect. The text was written about 1100, shortly after Matilda's marriage and coronation. The intentions of both commissioner and craftsman fit perfectly together and are accomplished in the creation of this artifact, the *Vita Margaritae.* Such a confluence of intentions

---

[11] I am aware that there is some scholarly debate over the actual authorship of this text. I accept the attribution to Turgot, but, in any event, a difference in authorship would not affect my theological reading of the text.

[12] The text of the *Vita Margaritae* is to be found in *AASS* 19, 328–40.

suggests that this text is marked by very particular reference not only to the life of Margaret but to the life and context of Matilda as well.

In general, the text is a straightforward piece of hagiography, of the sort written from the Merovingian period onward. In his brief preface, Turgot indicates his own specific understanding of that genre and of this particular text. He speaks of working under a double authority, that imposed by the present queen, Matilda, and the authority of Margaret's memory. "[O]n account of the authority of the one who commands it, and of the one whose memory must be expressed, I do not dare to refuse" (Prologue #2).[13] Turgot uses the gerundive form for the verb "expressed," which indicates the strong obligation imposed: the memory of holy things and holy persons must be recalled; it is both a liturgical injunction and the foundation of the Christian tradition. To remember God's action in the past is to understand the divine plan for the present and the future; to celebrate God's past actions by remembering is to ground thanksgiving (Eucharist) in the great deed of salvation.

By stressing the obligation to remember, Turgot connects this text with the liturgical and scriptural core of Christian faith. Appropriately, then, Turgot explains the parallel ways in which the Holy Spirit has implemented God's plan of salvation within the courts of Scotland and of England: the Spirit has inspired virtue in Margaret so that she reigned according to God's will. The same Spirit has also inspired Turgot to remember her life in the composition of the text, an action that furthers the implementation of God's will in the court of England. "For the grace of the Holy Spirit, which had given to her the power of virtue will, as I hope, give me help in what must be told concerning these things" (and, again, the gerundive form of "telling" reinforces the sense of obligation).[14]

Turgot then refers to several scriptural passages that give him confidence in writing; they also indicate his understanding of his task.[15] He

---

[13] "[P]ropter jubentis auctoritatem, & illius de qua dicendum est memoriam, contradicere non audeo" *AASS*, 328C.

[14] "Gratia namque sancti Spiritus, que illi dederat efficaciam virtutum; mihi, ut spero, enarrandi eas subministrabit auxilium," Ibid.

[15] "Dominus dabit verbum euangelizantibus: & iterum, Aperi os tuum, & ego adimplebo illud. Neque enim poterit deficere verbo, qui credit in Verbo: In principio enim erat Verbum, & Deus erat Verbum," Ibid., C, D.

recalls that God will give the right words to one who "preaches the good news" and suggests that, through the spirit, the Word of God takes flesh both in the person of Christ and in Turgot's narrative. The language and scriptural references in this introductory paragraph leave little doubt that Turgot understands his text to be in the tradition of scriptural texts. He explicitly identifies himself as one who preaches Good News and his narrative as a "proclamation." The same Spirit that brought about the Incarnation of the Word is at work in him; his text, therefore, will share the same source as the Scriptures and will have the same purpose, to preserve the memory of redemption carried out in a particular human context. Clearly Turgot intends his life of St. Margaret to be read as a theological document.[16]

In general, Turgot's narrative follows the usual hagiographical format. It identifies the subject, St. Margaret, Queen of Scotland, gives her royal genealogy, then, with the progress of her life as an historical frame, Turgot considers the themes of her sanctity. He carefully develops the characteristics of what might be called her personal sanctity—her asceticism, prayerfulness, observance of church practice—but also the sanctity associated with her status and public responsibility. He shows her as queen: contributing to the economic well-being of the kingdom, introducing discipline into the court, encouraging Christian learning, and taking responsibility for the reform and growth of the Church. These are all themes that one might find among the wealth of royal *vitae* that had flourished from the Merovingian times.

In one way, however, Turgot's work differs significantly. The earlier biographies of saintly queens gave limited attention to genealogical details. Of the many such biographies in the anthology *Sainted Women of the Dark Ages*,[17] for instance, most begin with the simplest sort of reference to the ancestry of the saint, with or without the names of specific ancestors. There is usually a very general reference to the goodness of her ancestors or, alternatively, to the fact that the subject of the biography excelled even her own virtuous roots. The life of St. Radegund by

[16] The similarities between Turgot's appreciation of a hagiographical text and that of Rudolf, author of the life of St. Leoba, are apparent.

[17] Ed. Jo Ann McNamara and John E. Halborg (Durham and London: Duke University Press, 1992).

Venantius Fortunatus contains a typical entry. "The most blessed Rade-gund was of the highest earthly rank, born from the seed of the kings of the barbarian nation of Thuringia. Her grandfather was King Bassin, her paternal uncle, Hermanfred and her father, King Bertechar. But she surpassed her lofty origin by even loftier deeds."[18] Occasionally the ha-giographer will signal the future holiness of his subject by relating a premonitory dream on the part of her parents, as in the Life of St. Leoba by Rudolf of Saxony or Florentius' life of Rusticula, abbess of Arles.[19] Even more rarely, he indicates the noble ancestry of the saint by refer-ence to pre-Christian roots. Huchbald, a tenth-century monk of St. Amand, sets the life of St. Rictrude within a larger story in which a semi-mythic Frankish nation "migrated from lesser Phrygia and propagated its nobility from the royal stock of Troy."[20]

Against this background—of the general, the commonplace and the mythic—we must look carefully at Turgot's more detailed genealogy with its emphasis on very specific virtues of named ancestors. In the ge-nealogy, Turgot does not give a typical catalog of Margaret's virtues, nor does he focus on the virtues particularly appropriate to women (though he later shows her acting in a stereotypically womanly fashion). In fact almost all of the ancestors he names were men. Among Margaret's many and notable ancestors, he holds up three virtuous kings and one virtu-ous count for emulation and praise: King Edmund Ironsides; King St. Edward, the Confessor; Edgar, King of the English; and Richard, Count of the Normans.[21]

---

[18] Ibid., 70.

[19] Ibid., 122.

[20] Ibid., 199.

[21] In emphasizing these ancestors in a text for her daughter, Turgot immediately demonstrates that he has Matilda's specific political situation in mind as well as her personal need for a mother's story. Perhaps the greatest "dowry" that Matilda brought to her husband Henry I was her royal ancestry. The Conquest was not all that far behind him when he became king; the integration of Norman and Anglo-Saxon realities into one kingdom was still a task that needed doing. Matilda's con-nections to the old Wessex line of kings as well as to both English and Norman nobility helped to reinforce Henry's dynastic status. It is not surprising, therefore, that Turgot writes only about the Anglo-Norman side of Margaret's royal ancestry,

In each of these, Turgot identifies a specific virtue that is revealed in the concrete circumstances of his historical situation. He notes that Edmund Ironsides was known for his "vigor . . . in fighting," which made him "invincible to his enemies." In contrast, he describes Edward as a "father" and a "Solomon," who demonstrated royal power and a prudent concern for his people by the way he made peace. Turgot implies that peace is harder to provide than even victory in war; it is achieved only by the kind of virtues that Edward had acquired: control of his "anger, contempt . . . for greed [and] absolute . . . free[dom] from pride." Turgot also writes of the virtues that come down to the good king Edward from his two grandfathers: Edgar, King of the English, and Richard, Count of the Normans. Turgot develops the portrait of the Norman Richard in some detail and even refers his readers to an historical chronicle, the *Acts of the Normans*,[22] for evidence in support of his virtues. He ascribes to Richard great energy for every worthwhile activity and a strong sense of identification with the poor, always remarkable among those who inherit both riches and political power. Richard was the patron of monastic institutions, to be sure, but he also participated in monastic virtues, taking his place as the lowest in the community, serving at their table, a model of silence and humility.

The legacies of both Edmund and Edward are royal gifts, beneficial only to one who is actually exercising royal power. They are not virtues of particular help to ordinary Christians and were not even noticeably evident in the life of Margaret as narrated by Turgot. By calling attention to these specific virtues, then, Turgot demonstrates that he is thinking in terms of the historical and concrete, of the demonstrated virtues of real men, who passed them in biological descent on to Margaret and then to Matilda through her. There is no explicit exhortation

---

even though she may also have been connected to the Hungarian Arpad dynasty, rich in royal saints. It demonstrates that he is shaping the text specifically for Matilda's use. The virtues that were given to Margaret by her Anglo-Norman ancestors and enhanced by her life have now come down to her children, particularly Matilda, newly crowned queen of the Anglo-Norman kingdom of Britain.

[22] "Cujus magnificentiae ac virtutum opera qui plenius nosse desiderat, gesta Normannorum, quae etiam ipsius acta continent, legat," *AASS* 19 329B.

in the text. But implied throughout this section of the narrative is the notion that these virtues have been passed on to Margaret, and to her daughter Matilda, as a legitimate legacy and, like all inherited wealth, must be both preserved and increased. It is what one owes to the family. The notion of inheritance in regard to virtue is made clear in two specific bits of text that require closer attention.

Early in chapter 1, Turgot affirms that before he can speak about the nobility of Margaret's mind, focused on Christ, and about the way in which she illuminated the following age, he is required to say something about "what went before."[23] He then proceeds immediately to discuss her ancestors. Turgot insists that the story of her many virtues will be clearly understood only if the reader knows about her ancestors, illustrious for their virtue. This is the usual distinction between nature and grace but such distinction does not imply antithesis. Rather, he implies a causal connection between the virtues of Margaret's ancestors and her own, saying that only in the light of the former will the latter be understood.

A second important passage comes just a little later in the same paragraph. Turgot is writing about King Edward and he describes his virtues thus. "He had a spirit victorious over anger, contemptuous of greed, absolutely free from pride. It is not to be wondered at, for just as he succeeded to the glory of his authority from his ancestors, so also did he succeed to a life of honest virtue, as if it were a kind of inheritance in law."[24] Turgot first gives a succinct and powerful list of Edward's virtues; they are not typical royal virtues, not the topoi of Christian ascetical literature. Rather they are unusual not just for a king but also for any aristocratic knight of that day. The primary activity of knights was fighting, and kings generally were those who could fight better even than their own knights. In that milieu, Edward's restraint from the common vices of his class—anger, greed and pride—is simply remarkable. But it is not entirely without explanation.

---

[23] "Quoniam igitur de illius, quam in Christo habuerat, mentis nobilitate mihi est dicendum; de illa quoque, qua secundum saeculum claruerat, videtur aliquid praemittendum," Ibid., 328f.

[24] "Nec mirum: nam sicut a majoribus gloriam dignitatis; ita vitam quoque honestatis quodam quasi hereditario jure est assecutus," Ibid.

Edward had inherited from his ancestors both the glory of his royal status and the "honesty" of his life (in Medieval Latin and Middle English, "honesty" is a synonym for virtue). Turgot sets up a grammatical parallel to express the likeness and equality between the "authority" that Edward had inherited from his ancestors and "the life of honest virtue" that he exhibited and to which he also succeeded. Turgot then explicitly affirms that his virtues, as well as his royal authority, were "an inheritance in law" or, in other words, the most uncontestable inheritance possible.

One final brief word about the language of the text. The various ancestors of Queen Margaret are consistently compared to one another in such a way as to imply that such a judgment is both appropriate and necessary. It is appropriate to ask how a descendent has used the inheritance that has been bequeathed; therefore, one may be also legitimately be compared to one's forbears in the matter of virtue. Edward, for instance, did not in any way "degenerate" *(in nullo degeneravit)* from the fame and excellence of his ancestors. He did not waste his inheritance, but added to it. The use of the word *degeneratio* makes for a strong statement; it is organic language, implying the living realities of personhood and, even suggests the biological dimension of humanity. St. Margaret, likewise, "adorned the famous line of her ancestors with the brightness of her merits" (p. 329 B). The relationship between various generations of virtuous people is thus described in causal terms and within an organic framework.

What the text presents, then, is an extended genealogy in which the virtues of specific historical ancestors are described as the necessary introduction to the present saintly subject. There are suggestions in this text that virtue, not just generic goodness, but very specific examples of virtue, can be inherited in a way similar to the inheritance of royal honors, dignity, and responsibility. Thus, successive generations of people are described as accountable to their biological forbears for adding to or squandering the patrimony of virtue. All of this together speaks of a notion, at least implicit, of inherited virtue.

The Theological Conversation Continued:
Ælred's *Genealogy of the English Kings*

A second text, intimately related to the Turgot's life of Margaret, supports this reading. It is the *Genealogy of the English Kings* written by Ælred of Rievaulx between 1153 and 1154 as a letter to Henry Plantagenet.

The latter had become, in quick succession, the Duke of Normandy, the Count of Anjou, the husband of Eleanor, Duchess of Aquitaine, and the designated successor to Stephen, King of England and to honor as well as to challenge him Ælred wrote a long genealogy of his own ancestors: biblical, mythical and biological. Ælred would have known Turgot's life of St. Margaret. Margaret's son David, who became King of Scotland after her death, was Ælred's longtime friend and mentor, and the latter begins his letter to Henry with a narrative-lamentation of David as the perfect king.

St. Margaret herself features prominently in Ælred's genealogy; he stresses Henry's connection to the earlier English kings precisely through her, his own great grandmother. Neither the life of St. Margaret nor Ælred's text utilizes the table form of genealogy; both are narrative in structure, giving vignettes that expose a particular virtue as a legacy to royal progeny. Both single out some of the same historical figures and both are written to challenge newly enthroned Norman rulers to Christian ideals of kingship that build on what are perceived to be specifically English royal virtues. I do not mean to suggest that there is a textual dependence of Ælred's text upon Turgot's, but I do suspect that there is a kind of theological dependence.

Let us examine several short passages in which Ælred suggests that he indeed entertains the notion that virtue, or at least the propensity toward virtue, may be inherited from one's ancestors. The first comes at the very head of the text. "So much is virtue in conformity with nature," Ælred writes, "and vice contrary to nature that even the vicious man praises and approves virtue; moreover, the vicious man does not excuse vice if he follows the judgment of human reason."[25] Then he points out that vice is always done in secret and darkness "as if it were embarrassed because of its innate degradation,"[26] while virtue is only hidden through humility. He goes on to say that "seeing that the love of virtues and the hatred of vices belong naturally to the rational soul, whoever devotes

---

[25] "Adeo secundum naturam virtus est, vitium contra naturam, ut virtutem laudet et approbet etiam vitiosus, vitium vero, si humanae rationis sequatur judicium, nec vitiosus excuset." *PL* 195. cols. 711D–712D.

[26] "quasi semetipsum ob innatam sibi turpitudinem erubescens," Ibid.

himself to developing a good character and virtues easily entices everyone and inclines their affection to himself."[27]

Here, the line of his reasoning and his motives are patent and quite simple. He argues, first, that virtue belongs to human nature while vice is contrary to it and he demonstrates this by two universal human characteristics. Everyone, even the vicious person, approves of virtue and disapproves of vice and, in consequence, people hide their vicious deeds in darkness and secrecy and let their virtuous deeds be manifest, unless they are motivated by profound humility.

Second, he argues that, since virtue is universally approved, all people are drawn to the virtuous person by natural affection. Appropriately, then, does he begin his letter to Henry with this passage. The young king, a well-educated man, has already demonstrated that he wants people to like him and this is an ambiguous character trait, to be sure, especially in a powerful ruler. Ælred appeals to Henry's intellect with a bit of natural philosophy and to his desire for affection by proposing that a virtuous character is most likely to evoke that affection. We can observe Ælred's rhetoric here. In speaking of the naturalness of virtue, Ælred says first that virtue is *secundum naturam* and, two sentences later, that virtue is *animae rationali naturaliter inest*. Both phrases mean essentially the same thing and the repetition creates emphasis. Of the several points Ælred makes in this passage, what he emphasizes is that virtue is intrinsic to human nature.

A little further along in the text, Ælred writes, "Considering from what lineage you take your origin, in truth I give thanks to the Lord my God because a son conformable to such origins has begun to shine like some new brightness, in whom the virtues of all the ancestors came together; I especially rejoice that the spirit of the most Christian king David has rested upon you."[28] Ælred introduces this passage with a long

---

[27] "Quoniam igitur animae rationali naturaliter inest amor virtutum, odium vitiorum, quicunque bonis moribus virtutique studuerit, facile sibi omnium illicit et inclinat affectum," Ibid., 712D–713A.

[28] "Ego vero considerans de quorum progenie originem duxeris, gratias [ago] Domino Deo meo quod pro talibus talis nobis filius, quasi novus quidam splendor, illuxit, in quo cum omnium antecessorum virtutes convenerint, maxime tamen in te spiritum Christianissimi regis David gaudeo quievisse," Ibid., 713B.

list of Henry's actions in achieving the throne, actions that demonstrate both restraint in the normal violence of warfare and generosity in the pacification of the countryside. Henry has restrained his forces from pillage and been "economical in slaughter;" he has protected the poor when he could and shown reverence toward priests.

It is this behavior—military and royal as his vocation requires but exhibiting also the virtues of wisdom, self-control and gravity—that demonstrates his lineage. In other words, from his bloodline the new king has received not only the vocation and privilege of kingship but the virtues necessary to its proper exercise. Thus he is one "in whom the virtues of all the ancestors come together," and he has shown himself to be a "son conformable to such [royal] origins." In this last phrase, the word that I have translated as "origins" is, in fact, *talea,* which means "a slip" or a "cutting" that has been taken from the mother-plant and planted independently. The suggestion is that Henry has been given an independent life and kingdom, but that he demonstrates by his actions that he is identical to the original plant. The organic nature of this botanical image, like the similar one in the life of St. Margaret, reinforces the idea that his virtuous actions—or at least the propensity for them— have a natural source in his ancestry. Thus, when Ælred, moved by his reference to David, interrupts his genealogical reflections to pen a lament for David, he declares that he intends the lament also for Henry, whom he "receives as the heir of his [David's] piety."[29] Henry is related to David by blood and by the piety that comes to him through that blood.

Ælred's language and thinking here owe a great deal to the stoic understanding of human nature and virtue, which informed Christian theology from its earliest days as part of the neo-Platonic legacy.[30] That legacy was reclaimed in new and vital ways in the twelfth century and significantly influenced Ælred and the other Cistercian theologians. In the Stoic system, all of the cosmos was composed of passive matter and an informing spirit, which was *logos,* the term that Stoics used to denote divinity immanent in the cosmos and, indeed, its governing principle.

---

[29] "te quasi pietatis illius haeredem," Ibid., 713C.

[30] I am indebted for this insight to Dr. Mary Beth Ingham, C.S.J., professor of philosophy and associate academic vice president of Loyola Marymount University.

The human soul was understood as a spark of the divine *logos* and, hence, the human soul was rational, indeed a participation in the divine reason. Virtue was human action that was consistent with reason and was therefore natural to the human person. To pursue the good, a person need only act in accordance with his or her interior nature, with reason, and such natural behavior was virtue. Nature is the model of all reality and hence all reality is rational, organic and dynamic, moving according to its own inner fire.

This principle underlies the imagery that Ælred employs throughout. The human person, to be happy, must only act rationally, in harmony with all of nature. There is no evil outside oneself; evil comes from human freedom of choice. Stoic ethics is all about choices; it is decidedly voluntaristic. But the capacity to make the right choice is inherent in one's nature and virtue is the natural expression of one's inner reality. Stoic anthropology is thus dynamic and optimistic; it was congenial to the Christian understanding as phrased by Augustine, that all human beings are *capax dei*. Since Christian theologians borrowed the language of *logos* to express the second person of the Blessed Trinity, Stoic anthropology was gracefully wedded to patristic soteriology, though in itself it was without a sense of the need for grace. Firmly rooted in the Augustinianism of the Confessions, Ælred's anthropology is based on the *imago Dei* model consistent with the optimistic outlook of the Stoics as Christianized by earlier theologians. Thus his proposal here of virtue that is natural and therefore a matter of one's human inheritance is not an aberration. It is completely consistent with traditional Christian anthropology. Unfortunately, however, it would be almost completely overshadowed by the emerging dominance of the Aristotelian understanding of virtue as learned behavior.

Finally, when Ælred does get to the genealogy itself—some 220 lines into the text!—he introduces it by a paragraph that bears heavily upon my thesis. I cite in full:

> Since we have described a few things concerning the excellent character of the religious king David, I thought it worthy briefly and truthfully to weave together his genealogy—which is also yours, most excellent Duke Henry—in order that when you see how much goodness there was in your ancestors, how much virtue was innate in them, how the splendor of their piety gleamed out, you will recognize also how natural

it is for you to abound in riches, to flourish in virtue, to be illustrious in victories and—what is more important than all of these—to shine in the Christian religion and the prerogatives of justice. For the greatest incentive in obtaining the best character is to know that one has deserved the nobility of blood from all the best ancestors. An honorable mind is always ashamed to be found degenerating from a glorious family since it is against the nature of things for a good root to sprout forth bad fruit.[31]

Note, first, that Ælred very carefully points out that David's ancestors are Henry's as well. This genealogy is not a symbolic one; Ælred does not simply pull out good English kings who might stand as exemplars for the young monarch as he seeks to rule the English. These are Henry's ancestors by blood and they have bequeathed him not only the rights and obligations of kingship but the possibility of virtue as well. This echoes Anselm of Canterbury's careful distinction between generic human nature and the concrete, particular human nature modified by human choice (see below, p. 38f.). Henry has not inherited merely generic human nature but a concrete, particular human nature, modified by the free choices of his ancestors.

Ælred does include some mythological or symbolic ancestors in the genealogy. Perhaps in imitation of the New Testament genealogies of Jesus, Ælred gives a more typical list-type genealogy that traces Henry's ancestral line through various mythological and biblical characters back to Adam. He interprets these as generic models for Henry by giving them allegorical, etymological interpretations. He notes, for instance that his ancestor Seth replaces Abel and as Abel signifies the passion of Christ,

---

[31] "Quoniam de optimis moribus religiosi regis David pauca descripsimus, dignum duxi genealogiam, quae et tua est, dux illustrissime Henrice, breviter veraciterque subtexere, ut cum videris quanta fuerit antecessorum tuorum probitas, qualis in eis virtus innituerit, qualis splenduerit pietas, agnoscas etiam quam naturale tibi sit abundare divitiis, florere virtutibus, victoriis illustrari, et quod his omnibus praestat, Christiana religione et justitiae praerogativa fulgere. Est enim ad optimos mores obtinendos maximum incentivum, scire se ab optimis quibusque nobilitatem sanguinis meruisse, cum ingenuum animum semper pudeat in gloriosa progenie degenerem inveniri, et contra rerum sit naturam de bona radice fructus malos pullulare," Ibid., 716 B.C.

so the etymology of Seth's name indicates that he represents the resurrection.[32] Interestingly, about Adam, Ælred only writes that he is the "father of all."[33] He avoids the opportunity to warn Henry about the sin that Adam has bequeathed, probably because this is a genealogy about grace rather than sin, about English historical ancestors rather than those in the history of salvation.

Those historical ancestors are highlighted in the text by the way in which Ælred tells their full story and the lessons of virtue he derives from them. Ælred asks Henry to pay attention to the congruence between the achievements of his ancestors and his own accomplishments. When he recognizes the way in which his ancestors' activities have prefigured his own, he will be able to understand that all of his personal successes are a result—at least in part—of his natural endowment, his true inheritance. In listing Henry's accomplishments, the points of convergence between what his ancestors achieved and what he himself is doing, Ælred carefully employs parallel grammatical construction: "you will recognize also how natural it is for you to abound in riches, to flourish in virtue, to be illustrious in victories and—what is more important than all of these—to shine in the Christian religion and the prerogatives of justice." Riches, virtues, victories, piety and justice are all equally the legacy of his royal ancestors. Or rather, it is the capacity, the predisposition, to enrich himself, to gain military victories, to abound in virtues and to shine with piety and justice that Henry has received. To act upon this predisposition is both Henry's glory and his responsibility.

In speaking of the virtues of Henry's ancestors, Ælred employs a word that doesn't appear in classical dictionaries. The word is *innituerit,* a verb, the subject of which is "virtue." Virtue *innituerit* in Henry's ancestors and this phrase is put in grammatical parallel with another that affirms that "goodness is in your ancestors *(probitas fuerit)."* *Innituerit* bears some resemblance to the verb "to be born in" or "to be innate"; it also bears some resemblance to the verb *initio,* or "to begin." Either word would be syntactically appropriate in the parallel structure and would make sense of the sentence; both bear the meaning that virtue is

---

[32] Ibid., 717B.
[33] Ibid.

part of Henry's natural inheritance through the blood of his ancestors. But on this critical point the text obviously leaves some ambiguity.

Ælred ends this passage with a sentence that describes the delicate balance between natural endowment and human choice required by a theory of inherited virtue. For the obvious theological question in such a theory is "how does inherited virtue affect human will and freedom?" Or, to put it another way, if one may inherit a propensity or potential for virtue, how is that potential activated? The same set of questions must, of course, be addressed to the doctrine of original sin. Anselm is clear on this point: original sin is made actual through the free actions of human persons. We might suppose, then, that Ælred's answer will have something to do with acts of virtue that activate the virtuous potential inherited from one's ancestors. But Ælred is more nuanced in his answer, embedded as it is in his advice to Henry. He repeats the idea that, first, it is important to know that one has received certain blessings from the ancestors. This requires that one appropriate the memory of past deeds as an empowering force in one's own life. This will have two beneficent effects. On the one hand, such knowledge allows one to appreciate that one's achievements are due, at least in part, to the gifts bequeathed. Appropriate remembering creates a humble gratitude, the thankful awareness that one's powers are the gifts of others. On the other hand, the same knowledge acts as a powerful incentive to act virtuously, that is, as a stimulus to freedom. Gratitude can generate the desire to emulate the good deeds that have been done on one's own behalf.

The pattern that Ælred suggests is very like the pattern that underlies the Eucharistic liturgy and the liturgy of the hours that were the warp and woof of Ælred's life and spirituality. Therefore, this is not a voluntary program of life that relies on discrete acts of willpower, but a balanced rhythm of interaction between grace and human freedom. The memory of one's spiritual inheritance, appropriated in gratitude, stimulates human freedom to correspond with the grace that is given in the act of remembering. "For the greatest incentive in obtaining the best character is to know that one has deserved the nobility of blood from all the best ancestors. An honorable mind is always ashamed to be found degenerating from a glorious family since it is against the nature of things for a good root to sprout forth bad fruit." Since a virtuous family is intended by nature to produce virtuous progeny, the honorable person will act in accordance with nature and with the virtuous traditions of the family, lest he shame them and himself. For this view of inherited virtue, Ælred cites the biblical metaphor, itself another botanical observation of how nature works, about the quality of the root and the fruit it produces.

Let me sum up what I think Ælred is proposing in this passage. He is writing about Henry II's real ancestors by blood, not using ancestors as metaphors or types. He says that they have bequeathed many things to Henry, among them the possibility of acting virtuously and of being both pious and just. Knowing that they have left him this legacy will, on the one hand, empower Henry; he will believe in his ability to fulfill all of the obligations, royal and religious, which are laid upon him. In other words, he will believe in the grace that he has been given. On the other hand, the same knowledge will give Henry humility. He will not be able to claim those accomplishments as solely his own, but as part of his legacy from a righteous family. Finally, if Henry recognizes the line of descent that gives him worldly power and spiritual capabilities, he will be most powerfully motivated to live up to the standards set by his ancestors, knowing that he is both empowered and obligated to do so.

There are many points of contact, in addition to the historical connection, which allow these two texts, the life of St. Margaret and Ælred's *Genealogy,* to illuminate each other. Both are written for newly crowned monarchs in England and both employ extended genealogical material to exhort and persuade them to a high standard of royal behavior. In the earlier text, the possibility that important royal virtues may be part of a biological inheritance is suggested, if tentatively, a possibility made more convincing by its context, the many-sided courtly conversation about genealogy and inheritance. The later text, written by an important theologian of the time, expands upon the suggestions explored in the life of St. Margaret and speaks more explicitly about the capacity for virtue passed down by one's ancestors, an indication that the notion was congenial to the Christian anthropology current at the time, especially within the Cistercian school.

Both texts reflect an understanding of redemption in which human nature is an active and positive component, in which the general notion of the human person as *capax dei* is made specific to the human process of procreation with its emphasis on the flesh and biological inheritance. In this anthropology childbearing and inheritance are part of the divine plan, a divine gift from the beginning of creation and fully sanctified by the Incarnation of the logos who himself experienced human childbirth and was a beneficiary of human inheritance. Within these texts the human reality of human procreation and inheritance through a biological family is used as a theological category. These themes were developed, if sporadically, throughout the theological tradition, with roots in the New Testament texts.

Childbearing and Inheritance in the Theological Tradition

Within the gospel tradition, Matthew and Luke both utilize stories of the Nativity of Jesus and construct genealogies to support their theological portraits of Jesus as the Savior. In Matthew, the genealogy serves to point out Jesus' Davidic identity and suggests that the whole story of salvation, that begins with the Old Testament, is the necessary background for understanding Jesus as the Savior. There is also some suggestion of his identification with a sinful people, especially with its unexpected inclusion of women from irregular situations. The nativity story is a christological statement, stressing the intervention of the creative Spirit in the virginal conception of Jesus. In Luke's Gospel, the genealogy points to the Christ as the universal Savior whose genealogy goes back to Adam, the original progenitor. Christ is not just one with the people of Israel, but united to all human beings and the Savior of all through their biological unity in Adam. Luke also stresses the virginal conception of Jesus and the intervention of the Spirit of God, but also uses his extended infancy account to stress Christ's identification with the poor and the outcast and the ministrations of the women on his behalf.

In their genealogies, the evangelists Matthew and Luke propose, not a notion of inherited virtue, as such, but the importance of Christ's inheritance through human ancestors in affirming his humanity. But there is also present a kind of exclusionary motif: what is affirmed is that Mary's conception of Christ is not like ordinary procreation. Jesus is Mary's birth child but not Joseph's son. This could give rise to a theology of human nature that ignored or depreciated human procreation rather than embracing it. In the Pauline letters, while there is a brief reference to Christ's birth from Mary as a means of affirming his humanity, Paul rather uses Christ's relationship to Adam, through human inheritance, in his exposition of the universality of sin. This would give rise to the tradition's reflection on what came to be called "original sin." Thus, within the New Testament texts, there were the foundations of two trajectories of thought on the role of childbearing and inheritance. On the one hand, there is the initial connection between human inheritance from Adam and the sinfulness of all humanity. This is the theme of original sin, which is developed from Augustine through Anselm of Canterbury and, in the fourteenth century, Duns Scotus. On the other hand, there was material for reflecting on the christological importance of human inheritance and childbirth in the on-going drama of salvation. This theme includes the affirmation of Christ's oneness with the human race and the universal ramifications of his act of salvation and can be traced here from the classical authors, Irenaeus and Tertullian, through a little known medieval author, Dhuoda of Septimania, to St. Margaret's biographer and Ælred of Clairvaux.

The Tradition on Original Sin and Anselm of Canterbury

Augustine was the theologian who most firmly wedded the notion of original sin to the biological process of human conception and procreation. For Augustine the fact that male sexual response lies beyond the control of reason meant that it was never fully redeemed. He therefore saw the process of sexual intercourse as inherently sinful and causative of the original sin in the human infant. The prestige and authority of Augustine meant that his negative interpretation of sexual procreation has haunted the tradition ever since.[34] But in the early twelfth century, and precisely at the court of Henry I, Anselm of Canterbury revisited the question of original sin and his argument differs in significant

---

[34] In the sixth century, Venantius Fortunatus elaborated on the moral dangers of sexual intercourse when, as Suzanne Wemple paraphrases him, "salvation hangs on a thin thread . . . with the panting of the breath and the heaving of the body [as] the womb swells with excitement and the serpent of voluptuousness grows." *Women in Frankish Society: Marriage and the Cloister 500-900* (Philadelphia: University of Pennsylvania Press, 1988) 151. The original text of Fortunatus is from "De Virginitate," *Opera Poetica, MGH Auct. Anti.* 4/1, 189–91 as cited in Wemple, 278, n. 3.

ways from that of Augustine. Anselm's thought seems to create an opening to argue for the possibility of inheriting virtue. He disconnects original sin from human procreation and thereby removes a certain stigma from sexual intercourse and the conception of a child, at least theoretically. He further distinguishes between generic human nature and individual human persons in a way that gives one's historic ancestors, as distinct individuals, a role in one's life of grace.

Anselm of Canterbury was the most important theologian of the Anglo-Norman world and his proximity to the court of Henry I could not leave him unaware of the debates about inheritance and genealogy that permeated the court. Anselm is best known to the theological world for a series of treatises that utilize new methods and, in that way, are precursors to the scholastic theology to come. The best known are his *Proslogion, Monologion* and *Cur Deus Homo*. But there is a kind of companion piece to the *Cur Deus* that seems to fit well into the contemporary courtly conversation about hereditary rights, the treatise *On the Conception of the Virgin and Original Sin.*[35] In this treatise he gives his own definition of original sin, describes the relationship between Adam and all subsequent human beings by which the sin of the first can be attributed to the others and makes a careful distinction between generic human nature and individual human persons that has important consequences for understanding sinful human nature.

According to Anselm, original sin describes the situation into which all human beings, after Adam and because of Adam, are born. The situa-

---

[35] Many influences helped to bring about the composition of the treatise. The celebration of the feast of the Immaculate Conception was the subject of lively discussion during Anselm's reign as archbishop (and, indeed, for a long time afterward; as archbishop of Canterbury, Anselm had undoubtedly been asked for his opinion on the subject and his answer lies embedded and implicit in his treatise. Anselm's treatise *On the Conception of the Virgin and Original Sin* most likely arose from his on-going engagement with the schools of Bec and Laon. Eadmer, Anselm's contemporary biographer, dates the *De conceptu* to 1099–1100. In her critical study of Anselm's thought, G. R. Evans has carefully traced the textual evidence for such the connection between Anselm's treatise and the theological questions found in the collections associated with Laon in the eleventh century, *Anselm and Talking About God* (Oxford: Clarendon Press, 1978) 182–87.

tion is one in which the human being has "the obligation of possessing, whole and unadulterated, the justice which it had been given and . . . the obligation to make satisfaction for having abandoned it"[36] but has also inherited a human nature incapable of satisfying these obligations. For Anselm, therefore, it is an impotent human nature, inherited from Adam, which, along with the obligation of the creature to creator, creates the situation that Christians name original sin. Following Augustine, Anselm stresses the nothingness (non-being) of sin. Strictly speaking, then, original sin itself is not inherited; it is the language that we use to indicate what is **not** inherited from Adam, namely justice and the ability, in justice, to give God what one owes God.

Furthermore, since the sin of Adam and Eve affected the whole of their humanity, body and soul, what they passed on to human persons is that human nature, modified by their sin. Therefore, in inheriting a damaged human nature, human beings inherit the "necessity to sin." What is not inherited from Adam continues to affect the existential situation in which all human beings find themselves: with an obligation to God that they cannot fulfill, the subsequent guilt of not fulfilling it, and a human nature that lacks the original integrity that would have made fulfilling that obligation both possible and joyous. This lack of integrity, which Anselm calls "corruption," prevents the sinner even from understanding righteousness and, hence, of preserving it.[37] Theologians will later develop a kind of theological shorthand for describing this situation, describing the effects of original sin as a darkening of the intellect and a weakening of the will; Anselm speaks of a "necessity to sin."

In the course of his argument, Anselm carefully distinguishes between personal sin and sinful or corrupt human nature. In fact, Anselm's argument depends upon a particular understanding of the relationship between nature and person, distinct but inseparable, in which the condition of the shared human nature significantly affects the individual human person and the autonomous actions of the human person affect the individual human nature that he shares. For Anselm, the mutual

[36] Anselm, *On the Virgin Conception and Original Sin,* trans., Camilla McNab in *Anselm of Canterbury: The Major Works,* ed. Brian Davies and G. R. Evans (Oxford: Oxford University Press, 1998) 360.

[37] Evans, *Anselm and Talking About God,* 133.

interaction between person and nature, held together in intimate unity, creates the conditions for the transmission of original sin. Adam's sin is personal to him, but in the existential human situation both person and nature exist in such intimate union that Adam's personal sin, which existed in his personal will, corrupted or damaged his nature in every respect.[38] All subsequent human beings inherit that damaged nature; but, again, the nature inherited from Adam contaminates their own persons so that they inherit, as well, a necessity to sin that becomes activated, so to speak, "as soon as an infant is rational."[39] It is important to affirm here that Anselm believes that historic human nature, which is passed down to every human being after Adam, is damaged and lacking, but it is not essentially evil. Sin, therefore, is never "natural" to the human person, but a rejection of true humanity, a rejection of that goodness that God intended for human beings from the beginning. Though Anselm is only concerned with the effects of Adam upon his progeny, we may, in fact, extend his logic and ask whether the actions of historic human persons, after Adam, have in fact modified the human nature they have handed down to their descendants. Anselm's understanding of the relationship between person and nature suggests this possibility and is congenial therefore to the notion that that human inheritance has theological implications.

Anselm's thinking on the relationship between Adam and all other human beings is shaped by Romans 5:12 and 19. In verse 12 Paul affirms that "it was through one man that sin entered the world, and through sin death, and thus death pervaded the whole human race, inasmuch as all have sinned." He repeats, in verse 19 that "through the disobedience of one many were made sinners [and therefore] through the obedience of one man many will be made righteous." Anselm makes a careful analysis of the implications of the Pauline text and, in doing so, explores natural evidence for the relationship between Adam and all human beings in the biological process of conception, as he and his contemporaries understood it. This in itself is an important methodological move. Anselm allows nature, expressed in the process of procreation, to interpret soteriological revelation, or grace. There is no distinction between nature and

---

[38] *On the Virgin Conception,* 379.
[39] Ibid., 206.

grace here; nor is one simply layered upon the other. For Anselm, both express the same reality, the existential situation of the human person and God's full economy of universal salvation. Whatever conclusions he draws from the biological evidence, limited as he is by the scientific knowledge of the day, he considers human biology a valid hermeneutic key for understanding revealed truths.

For Anselm and his contemporaries, the male seed, present in his body and therefore part of himself, is believed to contain the human beings that will come forth from that seed in the process of human generation. This is why the schools taught that had Eve alone sinned, she would not have caused the fall of the whole human race: the seed of future generations was not in her. But as Anselm has carefully distinguished between personal sin and sinful human nature, so he distinguishes between the personal existence of historic persons and their potential or proleptic existence in the seed of Adam. "Indeed it cannot be denied that infants were in Adam when he sinned. But they existed causally or materially in him, as they would in the seed, though in themselves they exist personally: for in him they existed as seed but in themselves they exist as individual diverse persons."[40]

Thus, like Augustine, Anselm links the transmission of original sin to the human procreation and speaks of carnal appetites as a consequence of original sin. He does not, however, follow Augustine by considering human seed to be sinful in itself, nor does he affirm that the act of procreation causes sin in the human person conceived. "Similarly, man can be said to be conceived of impure seed in iniquity and sin, not because his seed contains the uncleanness of sin or iniquity, but because from that seed and that conception from which he began to be a man he took on the necessity that when he gained a rational soul he would gain with it the uncleanness of sin, which is nothing other than sin and iniquity."[41]

Note that in Anselm's time (and as late as Aquinas), the fetus at the first moment of conception does not yet possess a rational or human soul. This was believed to be infused by a separate divine act at the instant of quickening, when the infant in the womb began to move independently. Note also that the seed, the material cause of the conceived

[40] Ibid., 379.
[41] Ibid., 367.

infant is not corrupt, nor is the biological process itself corrupt. Corruption or sin arises with the infusion of the rational soul, since sin is an attribute of rationality and volition. As soon as the soul begins to exist, it exists in relation to God, with the obligation to justice and the concomitant inability to fulfill that obligation that together constitute original sin. From this Anselm concludes that "there is no sin in infants at the very moment of conception."[42] The infant acquires original sin at the moment when he acquires a rational soul. There is, indeed, a sinful inheritance from Adam, but the mechanism of this inheritance is not an evil human biology of procreation.

Finally, Anselm carefully distinguishes between generic human nature and the concrete particular human nature of the individual in which original sin is actualized.[43] He introduces this theorem at each step of his argument. It affects, first, his definition of original sin. Based on the distinction between person and nature, he distinguishes between the personal sin of Adam and Adam's nature, corrupted by sin, as he also distinguishes between the inherited corrupt nature and the personal sin in every person who comes after Adam. From Adam, human beings inherit a corrupted nature; it is not possible, however, "to assert that original sin exists in an infant before he has a rational soul,"[44] that is, before he is a concrete individual. Rather, the soul is "corrupted" at the precise moment that it is united to corrupted human nature. The same distinction shapes his understanding of the relationship between Adam and all humanity. The seed of Adam is the cause of the individual, but while the individual remains in Adam, he is not yet a concrete, historic self. Anselm reiterates this point with awkward insistence. "In him they were not other than him, in themselves they are other than

---

[42] Ibid.

[43] See, for instance, chapter 23: "Indeed it cannot be denied that infants were in Adam when he sinned. But they existed causally or materially in him, as they would in the seed, though in themselves they exist personally: for in him they existed as seed, though in themselves they exist as individual diverse persons. In him they were not other than him, in themselves they are other than him. In him they were he, in themselves they are they. More simply, they were in him, but they did not exist as themselves, because they were not yet themselves," Ibid., 379.

[44] Ibid., 361.

him. In him they were he, in themselves they are they. More simply, there were in him, but they did not exist as themselves, because they were not yet themselves."[45]

Anselm's distinction between generic human nature and concrete particular human nature seems to leave room for the possibility that the human nature of a concrete individual can influence the way in which a human person actualizes original sin. After all, not everyone actualizes the universal potential for sin in exactly the same way. The sinful personal choice each makes is influenced by many factors, one of which is one's personal character. What human ancestors bequeath to their progeny is their concrete and specific human nature, that is, general human nature modified by someone's specific personal choices. Anselm briefly entertains the possibility that the sins of recent ancestors are to be included in the original sin that all human beings inherit.[46]

Although he ultimately rejects this possibility, it is not because one's more immediate ancestors have no shaping influence upon the specific rational will of the individual. It is rather because, in the spirit of Romans 5, the sin—the loss of the ability to render God appropriate honor—and the punishment—death—are so sweeping that there is nothing left to be lost by one's forbears. This argument does not obviate the possibility that some more limited moral good or evil might be part of one's human, biological legacy. The predisposition for a particular vice or virtue is simply not pertinent to Anselm's argument, which is, we must remember, about the possible theological basis for accepting the immaculate conception of the Virgin Mary. But his great care in distinguishing between original sin, rooted in a common human nature, and personal sin, a consequence of rational choices made by concrete individuals allow us to entertain the following working hypothesis: that an inclination toward virtue can be inherited from one's forbears, just as original sin, a lack of grace that inclines one toward sinfulness, has been inherited from Adam. In fact, given that Anselm is firm in his conviction that our human nature, wounded by sin, has not become intrinsically evil, one can say, following Anselm, that our ability for virtuous acts has been mitigated but not utterly lost. Human nature, however

---

[45] Ibid., 379.
[46] Ibid., 361.

wounded, still enjoys what the Scholastics will later call a *potentia obedientialis,*[47] that is, the potential for responding to God's grace and, therefore, the possibility to respond virtuously. If that is true of human nature, in general, then it would seem reasonable to assume that one's historical forbears can pass on, embedded in the concrete human nature they bequeath, the possibility for particular virtues.[48]

The genealogical observations of St. Margaret's biographer and the work of Anselm on original sin suggest real possibilities for a positive theological interpretation of human procreation and childbirth. If one's historic ancestors can endow one with the capacity for specific virtues and if the human nature one is given at birth is intrinsically good and has a God-given inclination for responding to God's grace, then human procreation and childbirth are, potentially at least, instrumental causes in the work of salvation. This marks a significant move away from the thought of Augustine and Anselm's position would be developed further by Duns Scotus who, in the fourteenth century, again considered the relationship between original sin and the teaching on the Immaculate Conception. Scotus will disengage the doctrine of the Incarnation from its usual relationship to original sin and argue that the motivation for the Incarnation lies not in sin but in God's freedom and unconditional love. He will demonstrate the possibility of a redeemed human nature in which human desire, including sexual desire, is good.

Like Anselm Scotus identifies original sin as the privation of justice, a condition of the soul and, while admitting the physical consequences of original sin, does not regard the body as guilty. While this obviously remained a minority position within the tradition, it is, nonetheless, within and not outside of the tradition. Yet it never fully overcame the negative attitudes toward childbearing that continued unbroken through the pa-

---

[47] The scholastics may well have benefited from Anselm on this point, in which case, the genealogical discussions at Henry's court provide some of the social background to the theological notion of *potentia obedientialis.* I am indebted to Fr. James Fredericks, Ph.D., for this insight.

[48] Father Fredericks also suggests that this is quite congenial to the thought of Rahner for whom "the *potentia obedientialis* is not merely some passive disposition of the human person to receive grace, if perchance grace should be offered" but rather "an active principle that positively orients the human person to grace."

tristic, medieval, and early modern periods. The sheer intellectual dominance of Augustine meant that sexual intercourse and biological procreation would retain their negative connotations even after persuasive
counterarguments of theologians of the stature of Anselm and Scotus.

This prevailing negative attitude affected the way in which the story
in Genesis 3 was consistently interpreted. In the text, childbirth is made
painful as a punishment for Eve's sin. Although the text clearly affirms
that childbirth was not itself a punishment, only the pains that would
thereafter attend it, nevertheless, Genesis 3 tended to associate oppro-
brium with all childbirth. The Pastor's statement in the epistle to Timothy, that "salvation for the woman will be in the bearing of children"
(1 Tim 2:15) was generally understood to relegate childbirth to a penalty
or penance that would be effective medicine for sin rather than an activity that is full of graced potential. Given the preceding verse 14,
which states that "it was not Adam who was deceived; it was the woman
who, yielding to deception, fell into sin," it seems that the Pastor uses
the Old Testament story to interpret the situation of the redeemed. This
exactly reverses the usual practice of Christian exegetes, for whom
Christ's redemption is the hermeneutic key to the Old Testament.

Patristic exegesis reveals that, when it was a case of texts about
women, the Old Testament strictures were allowed to stand and the salvific work of Christ was minimized. It is not surprising, then, that Paul's
reflections on universal sinfulness, couched in the language of what is
inherited from Adam, would come to be interpreted within the categories of original sin and in such a way that human childbirth would be
seen as contaminated. But Christian theologians also had the gospel
narratives in which the infancy accounts and genealogies were important elements in the Church's christological testimony. As the early
Church struggled to understand and express its faith in the Incarnation
and in the salvation wrought by an Incarnate Lord, the birth stories became part of the christological evidence. This brings us to the second
trajectory of thought and the work of Irenaeus and Tertullian.

A Theology of Childbirth and Inheritance: Early Patristic Contributions

By the middle of the second century in Lyons, the bishop and theologian Irenaeus was already pursuing themes that bear powerfully on
the salvific possibilities of childbearing and inheritance. In *Against the*

Heresies, he contests the thinking of those who have allowed their neo-Platonic convictions to undermine the full reality of the Incarnation; they have denied the essential unity between the Divine Word and the human Jesus. In Book III, Chapter 16, Irenaeus uses the Prologue of John's Gospel and the Infancy narratives to reaffirm that essential unity; he thereby makes the natural process of childbirth and the physical reality of Christ's birth the primary evidence of his full humanity. He plays variations on this theme throughout the chapter, using the language of "seed of David," and "the fruit of David's body" to emphasize how, precisely by his birth from a human mother and in a fully human manner, Christ is incorporated into the natural development of the human family, where genealogy and inheritance play a determinative, if limited, role. Thus he arrives at a summary statement of soteriological faith that emphasis the flesh of Christ. God's "only-begotten Word, who is always present with the human race, united to and mingled with His own creation, according to the Father's pleasure, and who became flesh, is Himself Jesus Christ our Lord, who did also suffer for us, and rose again on our behalf, and who will come again in the glory of His Father, to raise up all flesh and for the manifestation of salvation. . . ."[49]

In this synthetic statement, the flesh is both the instrument of salvation, insofar as it is united to the Word, and its telos, insofar as Christ's goal is to raise up all human flesh from death. Having demonstrated that the generation of Christ from Mary was the completely human and natural process of birth, he then describes it as "a holy thing" and the beginning of a new order of human generation: "that as by the former generation [i.e., our generation from Adam] we inherited death, so by this new generation we might inherit life."[50] He does not make Mary's generation of Christ unique and exclusive, but rather the initiation of a new order of human existence.

Irenaeus' soteriology consistently follows the recapitulation model, with its emphasis on a new human race begun by Christ, in which the gifts originally given to Adam are restored and Christ "sums up all things

---

[49] Irenaeus, *Against the Heresies* in *The Ante-Nicene Fathers*, vol. I, ed. A. Roberts and J. Donaldson (Grand Rapids, Mich.: Wm. B. Eerdmans Publishing Co., 1979) 442.

[50] Ibid., 527.

in Himself" (p. 8). In drawing out the implications of his soteriology, Irenaeus stresses the way in which Christ's human experiences sanctify those same experiences for those who come after him in faith. Thanks to the full reality of the Word Incarnate, what Christ experienced in his earthly life—e.g., infancy, childhood, friendship, work, suffering—becomes salvific for those who believe in him and experience what he did. Irenaeus develops this understanding in terms of Christ's sufferings, which makes salvific the sufferings of those who follow his example but he also extends his insight to include the full range of his human activity. "For, in what way could we be partakers of the adoption of sons, unless we had received from Him through the Son that fellowship which refers to Himself, unless His Word, having been made flesh, had entered into communion with us? **Wherefore also he passed through every stage of life, restoring to all [stages] communion with God** [emphasis mine]."[51]

Irenaeus writes of the exchange of natures that takes place in the Incarnation and of the exchange of goods that follows upon it, by which divine life is given to human beings and human beings are attached to God and thereby receive immortality.[52] Since the flesh and blood of Christ have become the instruments of salvation, flesh is not excluded from salvation.[53] He continues to emphasize that human embodiment, "the flesh" as he consistently and pointedly terms it, is entirely redeemed. He brings this conviction to bear on his interpretation of death. Irenaeus does not deny that, even after Christ, the believer experiences the full reality of human death and the dissolution of the body "into the common dust of mortality." But he argues that the resurrection of the body is like God's original creation of humanity from nothingness and points out that, theoretically, it is easier "to re-integrate again that which had been created and then afterwards decomposed into earth. . . ."[54] than to create the human person out of nothing.

For Irenaeus the experience of personal death and dissolution is an example of God's "power made perfect in weakness," and a sure remedy

---

[51] Ibid., 448.

[52] Ibid., 527.

[53] He says explicitly that "the flesh, therefore, is not destitute [of participation] in the constructive wisdom and power of God," Ibid., 529.

[54] Ibid.

against the natural arrogance to which flesh is heir. Death unambiguously teaches us that we are creatures and utterly dependent upon God. It does not teach us that the flesh is contemptible or beyond redemption. If even death is not a sign that the flesh has not fully been saved in Christ and through Christ's flesh, then surely the experience of childbirth, however much it indicates human weakness and indignity, however intimately it is linked to human death (see Tertullian on this point below), is neither contemptible nor beyond redemption. The thought of Irenaeus certainly leaves open the possibility that childbearing, cursed for the sin of Adam, is fully redeemed by the flesh of Christ and potentially salvific for those who, believing in him, experience it. For those who would develop a theology of childbirth, Irenaeus leaves an important legacy. His soteriology emphasizes the birth of Christ from Mary as the primary evidence of his Incarnation; his development of the recapitulation model of Christology affirms the redeemed and redeeming character of every human experience.

Somewhat later, about 200, in Carthage, Tertullian again undertook to refute heretics whose philosophical presuppositions led them to disparage or deny the embodiment of the redeemer. In *The Flesh of Christ* he argues the reality and importance of Christ's flesh in the process of redemption and he focuses quite dramatically upon the reality of Christ's birth from Mary. If Irenaeus implicitly acknowledges the redeemed character of Christ's human birth, Tertullian explicitly affirms it. He confronts the heretic's repudiation of Christ's embodiment with a graphic description of childbirth that itemizes all that his contemporaries found undignified, even repulsive, such as "the uncleanness of the generative elements" and an infant "shed into life with the embarrassments that accompany it."[55] Human beings are born into this world through a biological process that neo-Platonic philosophers believed to corrupt humankind, or, at least, to be unworthy of human dignity. If childbirth were unworthy of human nature, it must then be alien to God and not to be predicated of the Christ. Tertullian reminds the heretics that God loves the human persons whom God chooses to redeem,

---

[55] In *The Ante-Nicene Fathers,* III, ed. and trans. Alexander Roberts and James Donaldson (Grand Rapids, Mich.: Wm. B. Eerdmans Publishing Company, 1976) 524.

and therefore must love the birth process since it is their source. And if human birth does not shame those who are redeemed by God, neither can it shame the Redeemer. Indeed, by experiencing human childbirth, Tertullian affirms, the Redeemer redeems it. "Our birth He reforms from death by a second birth from heaven; our flesh He restores from every harassing malady. . . ."[56] Tertullian explicitly draws out the way in which this reality reflects upon the childbirth that women experience. "Inveigh now likewise against the shame itself of a woman in travail," Tertullian challenges Marcion, "which, however, rather to be honored in consideration of that peril, or to be held sacred in respect of (the mystery of) nature."[57] For Tertullian, the woman in labor is to be respected both for the danger she undergoes and for the divine mystery in which she participates.

He garners scriptural support for his position from Paul's First Letter to the Corinthians, "God has chosen the foolish things of the world, that he may put to shame the things that are wise" (1:27). What can be more foolish, he asks, than for God to "wallowed in all the aforementioned humiliations of nature" that he has just graphically described? Tertullian acknowledges that in its original context, the "foolishness of God" to which Paul refers is Christ's suffering and death, but he affirms that the latter is built upon the former, that they are both of a piece. The structure of his argument suggests that, for Tertullian's adversaries, if not for Tertullian himself, the birth process is at least as shameful as death, if not more so. Indeed, following the philosophers, Tertullian affirms the intimate connection between death and birth: ". . . for nothing is in the habit of dying but that which is born. Between nativity and mortality there is a mutual contract. The law which makes us die is the cause of our being born."[58] On the one hand, this perceived connection between birth and death helps us to understand perennial misunderstanding of childbirth as a negative, corrupting experience. On the other hand, it reinforces the theological move by which what is understood about Christ's redemption of human death is extended to include the redemption of childbirth.

[56] Ibid., 524.
[57] Ibid.
[58] Ibid., 526–27.

Central to Tertullian's argument is the affirmation that Christ takes his human flesh from Mary and that her biological inheritance to him is the flesh that becomes, by reason of its assumption by the Word, the instrument of salvation. This point establishes the reality of Christ's human flesh (bk. 17), the point of his whole treatise and therefore Tertullian supports it with an abundance of evidence from both Scripture and human biology. Finally, at the end of the treatise, he explains why he has gone to such lengths to affirm the reality of the human childbirth through which the Christ received human flesh, an authentic human nature, from his mother and her ancestors. He has demonstrated, "what the flesh of Christ was, and whence it was derived . . . against all objectors" and thereby set up the foundation for presenting the arguments for the "resurrection of our own flesh," a theme he intends to develop in another text.[59] For Tertullian, the nativity of Christ through Mary, and Mary's biological inheritance to him, is the foundation and instrumental cause of the Resurrection, the central salvific event of salvation history. In his understanding, genealogy, childbearing and the inheritance of the flesh is integral to Christ's redemption of sinful humanity.

Like Irenaeus before him, Tertullian has recourse to scriptural narratives and affirmations regarding the authenticity of Christ's human birth, his inheritance of Mary's humanity. Like Irenaeus, he sees these arguments as essential evidence against the heresies that would deny or vitiate Christ's authentic and complete human nature. Both theologians claim that the flesh of Christ, his human nature, is the instrumental cause of our salvation and thereby leave open the possibility that human childbearing, like every stage and aspect of human life, is both redeemed, and potentially redeeming, for those who by being baptized become "other Christs" and agents in the drama of salvation. Even more than Irenaeus, Tertullian hammers home the physical realities of childbirth in the development of a tradition that was always in danger of ignoring them or judging them negatively. In the work of Irenaeus and Tertullian, we see theological arguments that might naturally have developed toward a positive theological interpretation of childbirth, bio-

---

[59] Ibid., 542.

logical inheritance and the role of parents in the on-going drama of salvation. That development did not, for the most part, occur.

Procreation and Genealogy As Theological Categories: A Medieval Contribution

But there is one other document, written by an early medieval woman, who anticipates the twelfth-century interest in genealogy as a theological category for promoting virtuous behavior. During the later Carolingian Period, when theologians were explicitly and actively concerned to promote lay holiness within the context of worldly obligations,[60] Dhuoda of Septimania, wrote a book for her two sons. Within her *Liber Manualis*,[61] the related concepts of genealogy, ancestry, and inheritance are transformed into theological categories for understanding religious truth and obligations. Like the charters of Henry I, Dhuoda's work deals, first, with the biological and material realities of genealogy and inheritance. Dhuoda, bids William, her older son, pray for his father's relatives for they "handed down their goods to him in legitimate inheritance."[62] She knows full well that worldly power and status inevitably involve conflicting obligations and loyalties, and Dhuoda therefore offers her son a moral program by which he is to negotiate the conflict between what he owes to family and what to his feudal lord.

Dhuoda also considers what the human race has inherited from Adam, as Augustine had done before her and Anselm would do in the twelfth century. But unlike Augustine and Anselm, Dhuoda considers how the common ancestry and descent from Adam binds human beings together in charity rather than in inherited sin. Dhuoda develops

---

[60] See Marie Anne Mayeski, "Excluded by the Logic of Control: Women in Medieval Society and Scholastic Theology" in *Equal at the Creation*, ed. Joseph Martos and Pierre Hegy (Toronto: University of Toronto Press, 1998) 70–95.

[61] The definitive edition of the text is to be found in Dhuoda, *Manual pour mon fils*, ed. Pierre Riché, and trans. Bernard de Vrégille and Claude Mondésert, SC 225 (Paris: Editions du Cerf, 1975). The English translation is Carol Neel, *Handbook for William: A Carolingian Woman's Counsel for Her Son* (Lincoln and London: University of Nebraska Press, 1991). See also Marie Anne Mayeski, *Dhuoda: Ninth Century Mother and Theologian* (Scranton: University of Scranton Press, 1995).

[62] Neel, 87.

this theme in the context of William's secular and spiritual obligations that he has inherited along with his status, wealth, and power. One of these obligations is the dispensation of necessary goods to the poor and in Book IV, Chapter 9, Dhuoda entreats William to "help the poor as you are able." Developing this point further, she writes:

> It is fitting that he who accepts at no cost another's goods should offer his own for free to the extent that he can. Therefore I direct you to minister with food and drink to the needy and with clothing to the naked. May each man [sic] give away with a smile what he knows is his. It is written, "Deal thy bread to the hungry, and bring the needy and the harbourless into thy house: when thou shalt see one naked, cover him, and despise not thy own flesh."
>
> Here, the word "flesh" signifies the state of brotherhood in which all of us take our origin, as the first-made man himself said of her who was like him and joined to him, "This is now bone of my bones, flesh of my flesh." For "flesh," *caro,* takes its name from "to fall," *cadere,* in the sense and to the degree that the poor man as well as the rich may fall and rise again, but all are returned to dust in the end. Hence it is just that those who acquire great things through their merits should offer material sustenance and aid to such lesser persons of whom they are aware. In fraternal compassion—for those who thirst, hunger and are naked, to orphans and pilgrims, strangers and widows, and to little children and all the needy and oppressed—help them kindly, taking pity upon them whenever you see them. For if you do so, "then shall the light break forth as the morning," and brightness shine upon your steps everywhere. Mercy and peace will never desert you, and everywhere, through all time, truth and justice shall go before thy face.[63]

William has not personally acquired his own wealth; having received it as an inheritance of his biological ancestors, he is obligated to share it generously. Dhuoda then explains how the notion of human flesh shapes a Christian's attitude to others, especially in the distribution of wealth. For her, "flesh" refers, first, to the "state of brotherhood" that is our common inheritance from Adam. It is the flesh of Adam, his body, that is the common physical patrimony of all humankind and this biological reality becomes, for Dhuoda, the basis of so-

---

[63] Ibid., 62–63.

cial responsibilities that extend to the entire human race. She cites Genesis 2:23, "You are bone of my bones, flesh of my flesh," a text used consistently to explain the God-given purpose of marriage, thus underlining that it is through sexual union sanctified in marriage that the common patrimony of the body is transmitted. In giving one of her many erroneous etymologies, she does link "flesh" to its frailty, but for her the frailty of human embodiment has little or nothing to do with any religious contempt for the body nor original sin but rather to the ordinary social rhythms of human affairs. In the temporal order, men and women sometimes rise in social importance and in riches and then they lose both again, often through no personal fault or even political failure. She puts these two truths together. On the one hand, human embodiment means that all people are biologically related to one another, all are family, since all come from one set of parents through the long history of human sexual union. On the other hand, the frailty of human flesh is revealed in the inexorable rhythms of social influence; all human beings are vulnerable to the effects of changing political forces and systems that allot great riches to some while many others suffer penury.

From the conjunction of these truths come William's particular moral obligations. Having inherited the means to right the balance, not because of his own goodness but through the fortunes of blood and political inheritance, William is obligated "in fraternal compassion" to share his wealth with others, "those who thirst, hunger and are naked, to orphans and pilgrims, strangers and widows, and to little children and all the needy and oppressed." This is what is inherited from Adam: familial bonds that extend to the whole human race and obligations, in justice and charity, to care for all members of the extended family. In Dhuoda's work, childbearing and inheritance become the basis for the moral structures of human society.

This idea reappears in a letter of Peter Damian about marriage, consanguinity, and church property. Just a century before Anselm and the Margaret biography, Damian posits a similar divine purpose for marriage and procreation; he suggests that as "God meant humans to be united by mutual charity, so he made sure they were united by common descent. When blood relationship becomes too remote, it ceases to perform this function of promoting charity between humans, and at this point marriage takes over."[64] For Peter Damian, the understanding of our common descent from Adam, central to Dhuoda's understanding of moral obligations, is too remote to be effective in the development of Christian charity. Marriage becomes the structure that supports the development of the bonds of charity by constructing new relational bonds between more distantly related persons. It introduces a new category of biological relationship to strengthen that which binds all human beings together through descent from Adam and Eve. Both chronologically and thematically, Peter Damian, with his echoes of the ninth century Dhuoda, brings us back to the texts with which we began of Turgot's life of St. Margaret, a renewed interest in the importance of genealogy and the possibility of inherited virtue.

Conclusion

"So the Word became flesh and made his home among us, and we saw his glory, such glory as befits the Father's only Son, full of grace and truth" (John 1:14). In this christological affirmation from the Fourth Gospel, the word of God and human flesh embrace one another in a wedding of opposites that has burned ever after at the heart of Christian faith. In the "Word" is encompassed all that the Godhead is and wills— creative energy and unconditional love without limit—and it is revealed in and through human flesh, which cannot thereafter remain unchanged or alienated from the divine plan. The glory of God, which is God's radiant presence, is full of grace and truth; it is the norm by which all reality is perceived and understood and, hence, it is the truth. It is the gracious condescension of God, through which all those who accept it are redeemed. This grace, this truth, this glory is revealed in the human flesh of Christ and human flesh is forever changed by its assumption by the word of God.

This reality of the Incarnation is at the heart of the narrative life of St. Margaret of Scotland and all of the other texts that we have brought to bear upon its interpretation. In the court of Henry I, where all the rami-

---

[64] D. L. Avray, "Peter Damian, Consanguinity and Church Property" in *Intellectual Life in the Middle Ages: Essays Presented to Margaret Gibson,* ed. Lesley Smith and Benedicta Ward (London: The Hambledon Press, 1992) 73.

fications of genealogical inheritance were being explored, Margaret's biographer reflects on her legacy of virtue. What is revealed in Margaret's flesh, inherited from her royal ancestors, are the virtues necessary for a Christian queen. But they do not come to her through some extraordinary visitation of divine power or revelation; the capacity for royal virtues is her rightful inheritance and she has in turn passed them on to Matilda. Redeemed by Christ, the flesh of Margaret's ancestors becomes the means by which she is given her flesh as the means of salvation.

What she inherits, according to the thinking of Anselm, is a human nature, damaged from its inception through the sin of Adam, but not vitiated of all natural goodness and capable of responding to God's grace, which she receives in baptism. She comes into the world with an obligation to God, as God's creature, but with a human nature that lacks the integrity, because of Adam's sin, to adequately fulfill that obligation. Nonetheless, she receives from Adam through her human ancestors a human nature that is created in God's image, with God as its telos and a natural inclination to move toward God. Virtue is natural to her. As Ælred insists to Henry II, virtue is the fulfillment of her nature and behavior that her reason both dictates and enables. Virtue is natural to her, insofar as she has inherited the fullness of human nature, and it is natural to her as a legacy from her immediate ancestors. Furthermore, the human nature that she inherits is not generic but historic and concrete, made specific by her ancestors and by her own individually created soul; therefore her capacity for God and for virtuous action is specific to her. Her virtues are those of a Christian queen, ruling in a late tenth-century kingdom that has received the Gospel of Christ. They include vigor and perseverance in fighting for justice as well as wisdom and prudence in making peace among peoples. She also inherits a special kind of temperance by which she is able to control anger, greed and pride even when, as a queen, she is in the position to exercise coercive power and fulfill her own unrestrained ambitions. The Norman Richard has bequeathed her an inclination toward humility and service and an example of how royalty can exercise such virtues. These virtues are part of her human legacy and in the exercise of her reason in enacting them she will fulfill God's will for Scotland and find her own happiness.

A weakened human nature and an obligation to God are not all that Margaret inherits from Adam. From him, also, she has inherited a biological kinship with all human beings and, as a queen, she has the means to care for the human family in justice and charity. The inheritance of wealth and power from one's immediate ancestors includes an obligation to recognize the wide range Adamic kinship in effective, just action. This is what Dhuoda reminds Margaret, Matilda and, indeed, the tradition. Adam may have bequeathed a darkened intellect and weakened will to all of his progeny but he also bequeathed the familial bonds that bind all human beings to one another. Marriage itself, among its other purposes and good effects, has the ability to strengthen these remote bonds of kinship with closer contractual bonds that can promote charity.

Through marriage and procreation, all human beings inherit a human nature that is damaged but intrinsically good, by God's creative act. Lacking integrity and justice, human flesh is in need of redemption and, in affirming the Incarnation of the Divine Word, the Christian tradition locates human flesh at the center of the mystery of redemption. Through the Incarnation, the flesh of Christ becomes the instrument of salvation and this has significant ramifications for a Christian theology of childbearing. "What was not assumed was not redeemed" was the axiom of Alexandrian Christology and both Irenaeus and Tertullian, though not part of the Alexandrian school, were firm in their insistence that, in being born of Mary in the usual way, the logos had indeed assumed the human reality of childbirth.

Irenaeus sees the human birth of Christ as the evidence for his full humanity, against the Gnostics, and the initiation of a new order of human generation, a "holy thing" through which we inherit life. In Irenaeus' Christology, Christ's normal human passage through every stage of life restores each stage to communion with God. For him, human flesh is entirely redeemed and every fleshly dimension of human life is both redeemed and redemptive. For Tertullian also childbearing and the inheritance of the flesh are integral to Christ's redemption. Tertullian's link between the birth and the death of Christ is a powerful affirmation, given that the death of Christ is always seen as the ultimate act of salvation. Both Irenaeus and Tertullian emphasize that Christ redeems even death and transforms it into an entirely new reality. Similarly, human birth, the beginning of human death rather than its opposite, is redeemed by Christ and becomes an entirely new human reality. To return to the Johannine proclamation, it is in the flesh of Christ, especially in his birth and death, that the logos of God is revealed, God's effective plan for salvation which exposes the truth about human flesh and experience and makes the latter the enduring means of grace.

Unfortunately for the tradition, later theologians neglected these positive and suggestive foundations, upon which a solid theology of childbearing could have been built. So too did they, for the most part, single out sin as the sole legacy of Adam to the human race, ignoring the potential for universal charity and justice that lay within the creation story. Thus procreation and childbirth continued to remain suspect and carry with them an aura of sinfulness and weakness not attributed to other natural human activities.

For the most part, Christian history tells a long, sad story of the exclusion of women. They are explicitly excluded from an active role in the life of the Church in the pastoral epistles and other scriptural texts. They were consistently forbidden to aspire to ministerial roles, to teach, even to enter the precincts of the altar. Positive admonitions to women privileged the ascetical life and a life-long commitment to virginity. A kind of grudging concession acknowledged woman's importance to the continuation of the human race and, in making marriage a sacrament, the Church sought to sanctify the married state and the bearing of children. But no solid body of theological teaching emerged to explore childbearing as a redemptive reality while liturgically a ritual of "churching" for re-incorporating new mothers into the worshipping community reinforced the notion that childbirth was morally and spiritually problematic.[65]

---

[65] There is a telling exchange of letters between Augustine of Canterbury and Pope Gregory I preserved in Bede's *Ecclesiastical History of the English Church and Peoples* Book I, ch. 27. Augustine's queries reflect the expectation that pregnant women or women who have recently given birth are to be excluded from worship, even from the sacrament of baptism. Gregory's answers reflect a more positive position. He explains that neither childbirth nor menstruation is sinful; rather they are natural processes ordained by God. Yet he also affirms that the pain of childbirth redeems the pleasure of coitus and acknowledges that the entire process of sexual union and the bearing of children is morally vulnerable. "For there are many things that are lawful and legitimate, and yet in the doing of them we are to some extent contaminated," trans. Leo Sherley-Price (Middlesex, England: Penguin Books, 1968) 80.

Yet in some few texts we see the glimmers of a more positive interpretation. We see an appreciation for one's human forbears as the source of the capacity for Christian virtues and the affirmation that Adam's legacy includes the universal kinship of all humankind. It is not unimportant that the texts that speak most powerfully to the salvific character of human childbirth and inheritance are rooted in the world and experience of women. When women were at the table where theological conversations took place, the redemptive character of childbirth and human genealogy were discussed.

3

Life of St. Leoba
by Rudolf of Saxony:
A Theology of Church in Mission

Preliminary Considerations: the Historical and Literary Context

From the fourth to the tenth century, one of the major tasks of the Christian Church, headquartered in Rome and heir to all of Rome's sense of hegemony, was the evangelization of the vast northern regions that would come to be known as Europe. Gregory of Tours in the sixth century and Bede, the Northumbrian, in the eighth left historical records of two major programs for that evangelization, records that were both narrative accounts and theological interpretations of the process of evangelization as it took place within the specific contexts of the Germanic tribes in Francia and those on the island of Britain. Toward the end of his *History of the English Church and Peoples,* Bede explains how various missionaries from Britain experienced a call to pagan tribes in Germany, ethnically related to the people of Britain.[1] Among these, one named Wynfrid was chosen by the bishop of Rome to undertake a mission to the Saxons living on the eastern fringe of the Frankish kingdom.

---

[1] Bede, *A History of the English Church and People,* trans. Leo Sherley-Price (London: Penguin Books, 1955) bk. V, chs. 9–11, 282–88.

Taking the name Boniface, this Saxon missionary was to become the Apostle of Germany. Bede understands this evangelical mission as a sign that the English Church has come of age, that it is no longer only a recipient of missionary action, but a source of it.

There were different perspectives on the process of evangelization and, in particular, on the relationship of Christian faith to indigenous culture, available in Bede's day and in Boniface's. Bede quotes in full the letter that Gregory the Great sent to Augustine of Canterbury in which the Bishop of Rome reveals a genuine openness to the culture of the Germanic peoples. Local pagan shrines are not to be destroyed but transformed for Christian worship; whenever possible indigenous celebrations are to be linked to Christian festivals and banquets in honor of the saints are to replace pagan feasts. Gregory was in favor of demonstrating continuity between indigenous religious traditions and Christian faith; only what was diametrically opposed to the truths of the faith was to be forbidden.

Bede's history is written in the spirit of Gregory's perspective. He reproduces Gregory's letter and demonstrates its wisdom in the success of the English mission, where local traditions were not destroyed, but subsumed into the Christian ethos.[2] The mission to Germany seems to have been carried out in this same tradition. In 735 Boniface wrote to the archbishop of Canterbury asking for a copy of the questions Augustine had sent to Gregory the Great along with the papal reply.[3] Later documents seem to show that Boniface did, indeed, bring to the evangelization of Germany some of the best traditions of English Christianity. In particular, Boniface treated indigenous traditions with respect and, where possible, with accommodation.

There was, however, another point of view on the viability of indigenous religious traditions, the perspective of Orosius, a disciple of Augustine of Hippo. Orosius wrote the *Historia adversus paganos* (c. 417), a work valued by Carolingian princes and bishops and cited by those who implemented the emperor's plans for Church renewal. Orosius specifi-

---

[2] Rudolf tells the story of an Anglo-Saxon's nun's burial in chapter 4 that indicates that her Christian grave followed the pattern of Saxon mound burials.

[3] See George Greenaway, "Boniface As a Man of Letters" in *The Greatest Englishman: Essays on St. Boniface and the Church at Crediton*, ed. Timothy Reuter (Exeter: The Paternoster Press, 1980) 40.

cally advises that all evidence of the indigenous pagan world is to be destroyed. Should someone insist on following the burial rites of his ancestors, for instance, he is to be put to death. Gregory the Great and Orosius propose widely different perspectives on the relationship between faith and culture and reveal significantly different theologies of evangelization. The texts of both writers were preserved in later European circles concerned with the establishment and preservation of the Church; this is convincing evidence that inculturation (as we term it today) was an important and lively theological issue throughout the eighth and ninth centuries. We are justified, then, in looking for further evidence of a theological conversation about mission and evangelization.

Narratives and letters continued to be written and preserved throughout the entire mission period that document each local church and its particular theology.[4] That the traditions of the English Church continue, with modification of course, in the mission to Bavaria can be seen in the collection of texts associated with that mission. Among these is the life of Leoba, written by Rudolf, a monk of the Abbey of Fulda.[5] Leoba was a nun whom Boniface invited to participate in the mission to Bavaria; she became his colleague, an important teacher, and a foundress of monastic houses for the Bavarian women who accepted Christianity and desired the monastic life. About one hundred years after the mission of Boniface and Leoba, Rabanus Maurus became archbishop of Mainz and undertook a massive evangelization project. He compiled commentaries on every book of the Vulgate Bible, began constructing churches in all the country districts under his authority, and commissioned Rudolf to write the life of Leoba, whose relics he also shared with many of those same country churches. In addition to promoting Leoba as a model of Christian life, Rudolf uses the narrative of her life to explore and promulgate a theology of evangelization.[6] She

---

[4] Thomas O'Loughlin, *Celtic Theology: Humanity, World and God in Early Irish Writings* (New York: Continuum, 2000) clarifies the importance of local churches and local theologies in understanding medieval texts from a theological perspective.

[5] Rudolf had been educated by Rabanus Maurus, who considered him his best student. Maurus, in turn, had been a student of Alcuin.

[6] I use "evangelization" and "missionary" interchangeably throughout this essay. I wish to note here that "evangelization" is of recent usage in Catholic circles and

had been central to the original evangelization of the Fulda region; now Maurus will use her life—and her relics—to deepen and extend the faith in the same local church. Rudolf also wrote the *Life of Rabanus*,[7] in which he presents the archbishop's missionary program in detail. He wrote his commentaries for the formation of his pastoral assistants, both clerical and lay; he provided the necessary infrastructure for the faith (churches) and trained those who will take the word of the gospel to the people as yet unchurched. Thus, the text of Rudolf's life of Leoba is not only a narrative about a woman deeply involved in the Church's mission of evangelization. It has also been composed to serve the evangelical program of a concerned missionary bishop, committed to the use of texts in missionary practice.

As Bede had done before him, Rudolf carefully cites the sources of his narrative; like Bede, he assumes that the historical authenticity of the events he narrates is important and that readers will want to have their authenticity validated. He names as sources four women associated with Leoba: Agatha, Tecla, Nana, and Eoleoba. As Rudolf tells the story, various monks from Fulda had written down the women's testimonies about Leoba; one monk in particular called Mago had even tried to make a careful study of her life and character, speaking to all of these women and taking careful notes. Rudolf complains that Mago died suddenly and left his notes in a terrible state. Nonetheless, Rudolf is able to verify the stories and even amplify them from the memories of monks who still live and who, in their youth, had heard the stories of Leoba from her contemporaries. So his narrative rests on the written testimony of her contemporaries and the living memory of those who had known those who had known her, especially the women who had lived with her.

The pattern of documentation that Rudolf so carefully provides echoes the first four verses of the Gospel of Luke and like the narratives

---

has been recently distinguished as the larger term, describing the entire work of the church in proclaiming the Word of God, while missionary activity is seen, more narrowly, as "cross cultural proclamation of the gospel." See the articles on evangelization and "mission" in *The New Dictionary of Theology*, ed. Komonchak, Collins and Lane (Wilmington, Del.: Michael Glazier, Inc., 1987).

[7] *PL* 106, cols. 39–64, trans. Dr. Jane Crawford, professor of classics and archeology at Loyola Marymount University.

of Jesus in the Gospels, the reliability of his text rests both on the probity of his sources and on the miracles associated with Leoba's presence, both in life and posthumously at her grave. The parallel between the authorial voice of Luke and that of Rudolf suggests that what the reader finds in the text is more than the narrative of a saintly life (or, in other words, not just biography). It is, of course, at the very least, Rudolf's interpretation of Leoba's life. The premise of this case study is that it is also a theology of the local church, an understanding of the life and mission of the Church in Saxony, rooted in the vision and experience of Boniface and nourished by the living tradition of the monks of Fulda until it finds expression in the episcopal work of Rabanus Maurus and the texts of Rudolf. In the pages that follow, the ecclesiology of the text is explored in terms of the missionary vocation itself as charismatic and institutional, the exercise of authority within the Church, the dynamics of word and sacrament and, finally, the Christology and anthropology of the text.

The Call to Mission: Qualifications, Charism and Ecclesial Acceptance

Rudolf's narrative[8] shows that the specific vocation of a missionary may be conferred in two ways. The missionary may receive an official invitation from the hierarchical Church as Boniface does. As Rudolf states, "The holy martyr Boniface was ordained bishop by Gregory the presiding officer of the Roman seat, who succeeded Constantine in the pontificate, and was sent to preach the word of God to the people of Germany."[9] Rudolf has significantly compressed the story of Boniface. In actual fact, Boniface had gone to Frisia as early as 715 on an independent but unsuccessful missionary journey;[10] he then traveled to Rome where he received an official commission from Gregory. After

---

[8] Rudolf of Fulda, "Vita Leobae Abbatissae Biscofesheimensis auctore Rudolfo Fuldensi" in *M G H, SS* 15,1, ed. G. Waitz, 118–31.

[9] "Sanctus martyr Bonifatius a Gregorio Romanae sedis antistite, qui Constantino in pontificatu successit, episcopus ordinatur et ad praedicandum verbum Dei Germaniae populis mittitur," Waitz, 125, ll. 37–38.

[10] In the spirit of the times and the tradition of Irish monasticism, such missionary journeys of individual monks were often understood as a "peregrinations." See Christopher Holdsworth, "Boniface the Monk," in *The Greatest Englishman*, ed. Reuter, 57–58.

two years in Frisia in partnership with Willibrord (719–721), he returned to Rome for an episcopal consecration before, finally, setting off for Germany where, with Charles Martel's support, he set in motion the missionary project in which Leoba plays her significant part. By compressing the story as he does, Rudolf is able to stress Boniface as a missionary officially designated by the institutional Church.

In contrast, Rudolf shows how Leoba was called to the missionary life by prophetic designation; indeed there are two prophetic experiences by which she is set apart for divine purposes. Like the prophets of old, John the Baptist and Jesus himself, Leoba's birth and vocation are foretold by prophetic dreams. Childless and advanced in age, her mother Æbba dreams of a church bell in her lap. Æbba's nurse, a woman "with prophetic spirit," interprets the dream with explicit reference to the story of Hannah and Samuel and predicts the birth of a daughter who, like Samuel, must be consecrated to the temple of God from her earliest days and "taught from infancy by sacred literature" (#6).

Accordingly her mother sends Leoba to the abbey of Wimbourne in Anglia, known for its learning and governed by the Abbess Tetta. Renowned from the beginning for her gifts for sacred learning, Leoba then receives a dream of her own. She sees herself with a purple thread coming out of her mouth; she pulls on the thread until she awakes from the effort of trying to roll the thread, which got longer and longer, into a ball. Leoba realizes that there is a mystery in the dream and submits it to an older nun known for her prophetic gifts. That nun interprets the dream as an indication of Leoba's call to proclaim the "mystery of the divine word" and prophecies that Leoba's ministry will be accomplished "far from this place, among other peoples, where it is necessary for her to go."[11]

The biblical elements in the story of the two dreams make their prophetic meaning clear. Like the Jewish prophets and apostolic figures, Leoba has been set apart for God's purposes from her mother's womb. Her vocation is twofold: she is to become learned in the Scriptures and she is to take her knowledge of the divine mysteries to far-off places. Indeed, the dreams identify Leoba as both prophet and apostle. I have

---

[11] "procul ab hoc loco in aliis nationibus erit, quo eam proficisci oportet," Waitz, 125, ll. 34–35.

demonstrated elsewhere that the tradition of prophecy had been slowly transformed throughout the patristic period and the early Middle Ages. By Rudolf's day, a prophet might be either someone who foretold the future or someone who was gifted by nature and grace to interpret the Scriptures in ways useful to God's people. Rabanus and many other theologians before him understand this ministry of learned prophecy as a genuinely ecclesial ministry, the institutional form of the charismatic prophet identified by Paul in his various lists of Church charisms.[12] Leoba is not a prophet in the first sense; she must appeal to another to learn what the future holds for her. But she is a prophet in the second sense. Rudolf is almost tediously repetitious in his attempt to show her skill in biblical interpretation and the time, talent, scholarly discipline and energy with which she studied the sacred texts.

But even this woman, generously gifted by nature and grace, must be given an ecclesiastical call and/or confirmation. When Boniface sends for her, the Abbess Tetta, prepared by Leoba's dream, understands that the invitation of Boniface is a revelation of God's providence (*divinae dispensationi* or "divine management" in the text); she sends her graciously, though not without regret, to the German mission. The dynamics of vocation are clearly laid out here. Leoba has been given the natural and scholarly preparation to be an excellent teacher (about which more will be said later). The call of God in her dream and the invitation of Bishop Boniface, taken together, represent both the intervention of God in her life and the official ordering of the Church to its official ministry. Both Boniface and Leoba are called to the missionary vocation by interior grace and confirmed in that call by ecclesiastical designation.

Leoba's missionary vocation is also confirmed by the life she leads as Boniface's partner in mission. She is responsible for certain important miracles that Rudolf perceives as confirming both the character of the missionary and the rightness of her teaching. In Rudolf's theology, miracles are occasions "of virtue" and in addition to "power" the word "virtue" also has in Rudolf's text an extended moral sense. When miracles are narrated, they are always intimately connected to the moral character of the one who performs them, whether living on earth or in

---

[12] "'Let Women Not Despair': Rabanus Maurus on Women as Prophets," *TS* 58, 2 (1997) 237–53. Presumably Rudolf shared his teacher's understanding.

the heavenly court where power is unlimited; the moral character of the missionary is itself a revelation of God's power to transform human nature and therefore both an attraction to and a validation of the message that is preached. Leoba's missionary vocation is confirmed by what Rudoph calls her "probity of character" *(morum probitate)*. The missionary, a public figure subject to the judgment of others, must lead a life that requires no explanatory gloss; rather, he or she must be radiant in exemplifying the message and doctrine being preached. The miracles that the missionary performs serve as unassailable proof that he or she is personally an authentic witness to the saving God proclaimed. They prove also that the teaching is itself true and can be depended upon to lead one to salvation.

In addition to possessing the necessary learning and virtue, the missionary must be capable of foregoing the strong bonds that bound human beings to their native land and culture. This is a particularly important qualification for Boniface, as narrated by Rudolf. The relationship between the missionary and the indigenous people is potentially troublesome and deeply problematic; the generous enthusiasm that moves the missionary to bring the riches of faith to those who do not yet have it too easily becomes both cultural and economic imperialism as later centuries have vividly demonstrated. On the one hand, the missionary is well advised to go to foreign lands supported by companions of his own culture. Boniface seems to have learned this lesson through experience. His first and unsuccessful mission was a solitary one; when he returned to Frisia with Willibrord, his countryman, he had a greater measure of success; when he is commissioned for his own journey, he sends immediately for companions from his homeland. Leoba, too, has companions from home: her cousin Tecla is part of her community and her countryman Torahbrahtum is the chaplain who attends her deathbed. On the other hand, the missionary must make a lifelong, faithful commitment to his new country and people; having put a ministerial hand to this particular plow, there can be no looking back. Leoba is presented as one who can endure separation from her homeland.

Rudolf mentions the Abbess Tetta's reluctance to send Leoba to Saxony; he mentions no such reluctance on Leoba's part. Twice in his farewell address Boniface reminds Leoba not to waver in her commitment to her new country and Rudolf specifically notes that "she was not mindful of her native land or her relatives."[13] Leoba demonstrates the firm and persevering purpose that Boniface required of all missionaries. Rudolf notes the vigor of her resolution and how "she exerted every effort toward that which she had begun."[14] Rudolf's presentation of her call and confirmation shows both a theoretical and practical understanding of the delicate balance between natural gifts, individual grace and institutional call that, together, make up a vocation to ecclesiastical ministry, especially in a missionary setting. The Church is poised, after all, between two worlds—the world of nature and the world of grace, the world of divine power and the world of human authority. As an institution, it must work out its apostolic mission with due regard for the authority structures that control its human destiny. Central to the ecclesiology that Rudolf presents, therefore, is the theological issue of authority in the Church: *ad extra* as it illustrates the relationship of the local to the universal Church and to secular authority; *ad intra* as it explores Boniface's use and sharing of episcopal authority.

Relationship of Local Church to Universal Church and to Secular Authority

1. Authority ad extra: *Relationships with Papacy and Court*

Just as one's personal identity is constituted by relationships, so the Church's self-understanding emerges from its relational bonds to the larger Church and to the established human community as represented by secular authority. Appropriately, then, Rudolf describes the local church of Boniface and Leoba as it functions in relationship with the Church of Rome and with the Carolingian court. In fact, Boniface's mission is part of a much larger story to which the struggle between Frankish political control and Roman ecclesial authority are integral.[15] The missions to the Saxons and the Frisians become both desirable and possible only when Pippin has regained control over the lesser kings

---

[13] "nec patriae nec suorum meminisset," Waitz, 126, l. 14.

[14] "omne studium erga id quod coeperat exercebat," Ibid.

[15] See Richard Fletcher, *The Barbarian Conversion* (Berkeley and Los Angeles: University of California Press, 1999), especially ch. 7, "Campaigning Sceptres: the Frankish Drive to the East," 193–227.

who ruled these lands on the eastern frontier of his kingdom. Simultaneously, the bishop of Rome was attempting, after the successful Romanization of the English Church, to enlarge his influence over the Frankish Church, which had developed along autonomous and idiosyncratic lines. By the time of Boniface, Frankish bishops and missionaries were often the pawns of the aristocracy and the ancient Gallic tradition of synods and provincial organization had significantly deteriorated. Boniface must carry out his mission under the reforming eyes of both Pope Gregory II and Charles Martel, each protective of his own authority.[16] Nonetheless, he also seeks to act with the authentic autonomy of the local bishop. Negotiating these potential conflicts required a clear but nuanced notion of church authority.

Rudolf describes Boniface and his associates as a "deputation" and makes a point of his official character vis-à-vis Pope Gregory, the "presiding officer of the Roman See."[17] The word "deputation" implies that Boniface acts essentially as a representative of Rome. From other sources we learn that on May 15, 719 Gregory gave Boniface a commission "to preach to the unbelieving Gentiles and this mandate is the earliest example of such a document that has been preserved;" the same pope consecrated him bishop in the following year. Rudolf telescopes both events into a single statement in his narrative and makes no further reference to relationships with Rome or, for that matter, of his interaction with other bishops. But, again, other sources tell of subsequent connections, not only with Gregory II but also with his successors. Over the years in Germany, Boniface received the pallium (designating him metropolitan of the region), initiated correspondence regarding the application of Roman practice to the new situation and swore an oath to promote Roman discipline in all spheres under his influence. There is significant evidence that Boniface worked in contentious circumstances where the primacy of Roman authority was by no means axiomatic; Boniface is its

---

[16] See Wilhelm Levison, *England and the Continent in the Eighth Century* (Oxford: Clarendon Press, 1946) 45–93.

[17] Gregory is described as "Romanae sedis antistite" (l., 37) and the chosen missionaries are those "quorum adminiculo iniunctam sibi legationem non segniter administravit," (l. 42), Waitz, 125. Together all of the missionaries make up the "legationem."

standard-bearer in the Rhineland and his oath involved him in a delicate balance of allegiances.[18]

But in fact Rudolf portrays Boniface's autonomy rather than his dependence on Rome.[19] He chooses and names others as collaborators in his mission and functions as one who presides in a collegial manner (about which more below), although he is both authoritative and decisive. He "decides" to go on to still-pagan lands; Rudolf does not say he is sent. Boniface calls Lul to him and commissions him as his own successor; such an independent decision of a single bishop was not entirely consistent with either English or Roman practice. A hundred years later when Rudolf writes, Roman hegemony is an accepted fact and he himself is part of its fruition, writing for a new archbishop sanctioned by Rome. Nonetheless, though he shows that the authority of the Roman See was instrumental in the German mission, he clearly shows an independent episcopal authority as well, giving effective leadership in and to the local church. The balance between local episcopal autonomy and the growing authority of Rome was both delicate and crucial. Boniface seeks appropriate sanction and counsel from the bishop of Rome; but he also acts as a self-conscious, fully empowered successor to the Apostles.

Relationships between the Church and the empire during the Carolingian period were also complex and often problematic. On the one hand, missionaries and bishops could not function within the Frankish empire and its dependencies without the consent of the rulers. On the other hand, church authorities were often obliged to struggle for sufficient independence to pursue their own spiritual and institutional purposes. Abundant documentation exists to clarify the ups and downs of this relationship during the time of Boniface and it has been dealt with in other places.[20] Rudolf presents a rather serene picture of the situation, noting primarily the way in which Leoba, the subject of his biography, fostered good relations between the mission and the various kings/emperors.

[18] Levison, 72.

[19] According to Yves Congar, *L'Écclésiologie du Haut Moyen Âge* (Paris: Éditions du Cerf, 1968), this is the common emphasis in western ecclesiology throughout the early medieval period. See pages 131–41.

[20] See, e.g., Levison and also Rosamund McKitterick, *The Frankish Church under the Carolingians* (London and New York: Longmans Press, 1983).

He credits Leoba's reputation for sanctity and wisdom with attracting the respect of no fewer than three successive kings, including the emperor Charlemagne. He tells how Pippin, Karloman, and Karl "cherished her with all respect" but that Karl, in particular, ruling alone after the death of Karloman, demonstrated an unusual degree of deference to her person and her opinion. "He so cherished the Catholic faith that, in contrast to the way in which he ordered everyone else, he entreated the servants and handmaids of God with high humility. He treated the pious virgin of God [Leoba] in this humble manner; with the greatest reverence he invited her frequently to visit him and honored her with worthy gifts."[21] Rudolf seems to imply that Charlemagne was moved by Leoba's holiness to an unaccustomed humility that ecclesiastical power alone could not induce. Rather, the Church's influence over Charlemagne was exercised, at least in part, through the saintly Leoba.

Other influential people shared Charlemagne's attitude. "Princes loved her, nobles supported her, bishops embraced her with the greatest joy. And because she was very learned in the scriptures and full of foresight in her counsel they used to discuss the word of life with her, discussing the business of ecclesiastical institutions."[22] Rudolf's affirmation may seem like hagiographical exaggeration, but her relationship with Charlemagne's court is well documented and Rudolf's readers would have recognized in his description of Leoba the operation of a powerful political role, that of royal counselor. Jonas of Orleans, a bishop much engaged in the political crises during the reign of Louis the Pious (814–840), wrote extensively on the role of the counselor.[23] Similarly, in her *Liber Manualis*, Dhuoda of Septimania,[24] writing just about six

[21] "Qui ita fidem catholicam diligebat, ut, cum omnibus imperaret, Dei famulos et ancillas sublimi humilitate veneraretur. Hic itaque religiosam Dei virginem ad se frequenter invitatam cum magna reverentia suscepit et dignis muneribus honoravit," Waitz, 129, ll. 36–38.

[22] "Amabant eam principes, suscipiebant proceres, episcopi cum exultatione amplectabantur. Et quia erat in scripturis eruditissima atque in consilio provida, verbum vitae cum ea conferebant et instituta aecclesiastica sepe tractabant," Ibid., ll. 41–43.

[23] *De institutione regia* on the role of monarchs and bishops and *De institutione laicali* on marriage and the obligations of the laity as an order within the Church.

[24] Ed., Pierre Riche, *Sources Chrétiennes* 54 (Paris: Éditions du Cerf, 1974). Trans. Carol Neel, *A Mother's Advice to Her Son* (Lincoln: University of Nebraska Press, 1985).

years after Rudolf's Life of Leoba, gave elaborate instructions to her son on his obligation to prepare for that important role. Dhuoda, the wife of one of Charlemagne's magnates, specifically addresses the tension to which a counselor is subject in balancing the conflicting claims of legitimate authorities (in her son's case, those of God, his father and his political overlord).[25]

Leoba, too, had to counsel princes, bishops, and the king so that they could negotiate their various legitimate but often conflicting claims, always giving the primacy to God's. Hence, Rudolf's emphasis is on both her religious and practical wisdom. In addition, he points out that she was loved by Queen Hildegarde, Charlemagne's consort, and became her spiritual director. This is not just a gratuitous note on Rudolf's part. In a period when the "court" was essentially a domestic reality and not yet a bureaucratic one, the queen was a member of that court with potentially significant influence on its policies.[26]

In Rudolf's time, as in Boniface's, the possibility for effective church leadership depended on the work of counselors. These were people whose holiness won them the respect of powerful secular leaders and whose wisdom taught them to negotiate the legitimate but often conflicting claims of spiritual and political authority. Carolingian political theory gave such counselors the official role of interpreting the will of God as expressed in the scriptures; they believed that, without such counselors, the political power of kings or the coercive power of the Church could easily usurp an authority that went beyond the bounds of legitimacy. Rudolf's ecclesiology, based on his interpretation of the practice of Boniface, promotes an ecclesiastical role for such a counselor, known for wisdom and holiness, who can bridge both worlds. Sought for her religious wisdom and perspicacity in institutional matters, Leoba the counselor was integral to Boniface's mission in Saxony. Through her,

[25] See Marie Anne Mayeski, *Dhuoda of Septimania: Ninth Century Mother and Theologian* (Scranton: University of Scranton Press, 1989).

[26] See Janet L. Nelson, "Queens as Jezebels: The Careers of Brunhild and Balthild in Merovingian History," in *Medieval Women*, ed. Derek Baker (Oxford: Basil Blackwell, 1978) 74–75. See also Jane Tibbbetts Schulenburg, "The Making of the Mulier Sancta: Public and Private Roles," in *Forgetful of their Sex: Female Sanctity and Society* (Chicago and London: University of Chicago Press, 1998) 59–125.

Boniface can hope to insure that his plans for the Church's progress and development are understood and approved by the powerful at court.

2. Authority ad intra: *An Early Collegiality in the Missionary Church*

If Rudolf presents Boniface as a local bishop who exercises legitimate autonomy in relationships *ad extra* and Leoba as an effective counselor who helps him negotiate these relationships successfully, then one must ask about the structures of authority internal to this local church. I will argue that Rudolf attributes a collegial understanding of the Church to Boniface and that this is a central, even determinative, theme of his text. He notes, first, that Boniface was sent by Gregory II as "*antistes* of the Roman Seat" (#9), a word that affirms Gregory as bishop, but makes no linguistic reference to his primacy. Certainly the title of pope was in full use already in Bede's day and in his circle (though it would be anachronistic to attribute to it all that the word later implied). Bede habitually uses the language of "the apostolic See" as well. Indeed, one of Bede's central concerns is to document the importance of the Roman traditions of Christianity and the need for the local church to be connected to and approved by the one who sits in the episcopal seat of Peter. At the heart of his history is the Synod of Whitby (664) at which the Roman discipline triumphs over that of the Celts in Britain; in the Synod debates the Roman position had been argued precisely in terms of Peter's identification with the Roman See. Therefore Rudolf's use of this rather different terminology must be noted.

Antistes means variously "priest," "overseer," or "presiding officer;" it was used in pagan circles to denote the chief priest at a large temple and, therefore, implies a kind of presider, coordinator, or executive officer of temple activities. In the Latin literature of the Fathers, it is used as an alternative to the more common *episcopos*. But we find it most often in letters, as the title one bishop uses in writing to another. Therefore usage gives it a quality of familiarity, or at least of peer respect. To designate Gregory as the *antistes* who sent Boniface suggests the interaction of peers. It may also imply that the diocese of Rome is led and administered by a number of different "officers," united by Gregory who presides over and administers the whole. There is no emphasis on hierarchy here; there is no mention of Gregory as Peter, the first among the Apostles (an emphasis dear to Bede). And since Gregory, the presider, sends Boniface as his envoy or delegate, it may be presumed that Boniface is to imitate

Gregory's example and preside over the local church as the overseer of many ministers. It is a genuinely collegial model of church structure, though the term itself is anachronistic.

A good evangelist, Boniface is clear about his pastoral goals. Those already baptized are to be strengthened by "constant exhortations;" those still pagan are to be "instructed in the faith" until they "eagerly flock to baptism" while the "depraved [learn] the way of correction."[27] The language of this description emphasizes a slow process of persuasion that appeals to both intellect and intentionality; it requires a long-term educational policy. Boniface also has a practical sense of the strategy of mission: first the message is preached to the "town" where the central church has been built; then it is extended "through the villages and farms." This, too, is a vision that requires both time and patience and, above all, intellectually trained personnel. Rudolf identifies the two methods by which Boniface seeks to accomplish the task: "doctrina salutari virtutumque miraculis," that is, "by wholesome teaching and miracles of virtues."[28] By "wholesome teaching," Boniface means more than exhortation or sermons preached to large gatherings and he intends that the people of Germany shall have a deep understanding of the faith they have already heard about. Therefore, cleric and monk, man and woman, all the missionaries must be equally "learned in divine law."[29]

It has long been acknowledged that the Anglo-Saxon Church placed a strong emphasis on an educated faith; Boniface clearly intends to continue that tradition in his German mission. He has no intention of converting people only in the minimalist sense of leading them to baptism. Rather, he "work[ed] for the establishment of a distinctive Christian culture in the lands beyond the Rhine and the Scheldt."[30] His contemporaries

---

[27] "Nam, cum cotidie populorum frequentia fidei sacramentis imbuere tur, divinus sermo non solum in aecclesiis, verum etiam per pagos et castella diffundebatur in tantum, ut [et] fideles catholici assiduis exhortationibus firmarentur et depravati viam correctionis agnoscerent et pagani fide instructi certatim ad gratiam baptismatis convolarent." Waitz, 125, ll. 43–47.

[28] Ibid., l. 43.

[29] Ibid., "doctos lege divina," Ibid., l. 41.

[30] George William Greenaway, "Saint Boniface as a Man of Letters," in *Saint Boniface: Three Biographical Studies* (London: A. and C. Black, 1955) 33.

understood this as his overall design; shortly after his death, Cuthbert, archbishop of Canterbury, wrote to Boniface's successor, Lul, praising his efforts in promoting a learned Christian culture.[31] Such a goal required generations of missionary work. In fact, Boniface himself is an evangelist to lands and peoples who have already heard something of the Gospel of Christ because they are living within the orbit of Frankish rule. But it has not yet taken deep root. Pagan practices continued long after Clovis' conversion, as Gregory of Tours bore witness, and they would remain even after the work of Boniface. That is presumably why Rabanus Maurus must undertake yet another mission to the countryside around Mainz, as Rudolf tells us in his *vita*, and why a theology of mission is still an important question for the Maurus circle of theologians. The work of creating a Christian learned culture, without which there can be no full appropriation of the faith, is still in process. Learning is still an evangelical task.

This extensive and intensive policy of evangelization is not within the capacity of a single missionary, no matter how charismatic his gifts nor how potent and spectacular his miracles; it requires wide collaboration. Upon his arrival in Germany, Boniface set about assembling the ministers who are to share his task, forming a kind of ministerial team (Rudoph uses the word "deputation" and, sometimes, "legation" probably because of Boniface's status as envoy of Pope Gregory II). He carefully balances his team, seeking both secular clergy and monks, men and women ministers, indigenous leaders as well as people from his homeland. At the same time, Rudolf notes that Boniface is a strong leader; it is he who ultimately administers the mission and it is not from weakness that he invites collegial support. It is rather with a sense of all that the mission entails that he invites the participation of others. In choosing the members of his delegation, he seeks qualified partners, capable of leadership. Given his pastoral objectives, he exercises special care to choose ministers who can provide leadership in his educational program. Boniface's collegium is representative in every way that matters to him. Even under the constraints of an urgent mission, he willingly takes time to select and gather those who will share it and to prepare his colleagues adequately for their task.

---

[31] Ibid., 33–34.

Undoubtedly following the English pattern, Boniface clearly envisions both a diocesan and a monastic structure as essential to the christianization of Germany and especially to its educational formation. He sent his student, Sturmi (a leader in the local church and indigenous in his cultural heritage) to Monte Cassino for proper Benedictine training and invited Leoba to come from Anglia as founder and superior of women's monasteries.[32] Leoba's full story, as Rudolf tells it, demonstrates the wisdom of these decisions: Sturmi's foundation of Fulda became the stronghold of the Bavarian Church and the seedbed of bishops while Leoba and her nuns form the spine of its educational strength. The name of Leoba's monastery is Bishofsheim, "the bishop's home;" he probably gave her his own dwelling as the core of the monastery to be built there. Such an action was a potent visible symbol of the bishop's incorporation of her work into his pastoral and ecclesiastical project.[33]

Boniface's collegial vision and, especially, his inclusion of Leoba as a member of the ministerial team, were not diminished or eroded by the practical experience of administering his mission. He did not move away from his ideal of collaboration, even when the conflicts and constraints of his mission grew burdensome. When he decided to leave the Mainz region for the still-pagan land of Frisia, Boniface called his colleagues

---

[32] Jo Ann McNamara has noted the importance of women's monasteries for effective and enduring evangelization. "Transformation of transient enthusiasm into a deeply rooted personal commitment to the principles of Christianity must be the ultimate goal of every missionary endeavor. Where there is no strong permanent local organization to tend the fire kindled by the preacher, it readily sputters out. . . . Monasteries of women, established first in fortified cities and later in the countryside, carried on this work in two ways. They acted as refuges to shelter women who sought to escape the confines of the secular world, and they acted as an evangelizing vanguard, reaching out to the local population." From "Living Sermons: Consecrated Women and the Conversion of Gaul" in *Peaceweavers,* ed. Lillian Thomas Shank and John A. Nichols (Kalamazoo, Mich.: Cistercian Publications, 1987) 25.

[33] I am reminded of the way in which Archbishop Silva vacated his palace on the central plaza in Santiago, Chile, to make room for the "Vicariate of Solidarity," an organization of Catholic lawyers called by the archbishop to work for the protection and civil rights of Chileans during the Pinochet regime. In both cases, the use of the bishop's house was a symbol of the real empowerment by the bishop in service of the mission of the church.

Lul and Leoba to him and commissioned both as his deputies in their respective spheres. Lul was to undertake the pastoral care of the diocese, while Leoba was to continue to put her knowledge of sacred Scripture and church law at the service of the mission, having special care for the women's monasteries (#17). They are depicted as partners in the fulfillment of Boniface's mission, partners with him and with each other. Indeed Boniface especially underlines Leoba's role as his own partner in his farewell address. He asks Lul to bury them both in the same tomb at Fulda "so that they, who with equal vow and zeal had served Christ in their lives, might await the day of resurrection side by side."[34] Then he gave Leoba his own cowl (#17).

This act, made even more solemn because it was part of a departure ritual, conferred on Leoba, first, a share in the power of Boniface's personal presence. Like relics, clothing contained the personal identity of the owner; by giving his own garment to Leoba, Boniface empowers her with his own personal authority. But the cowl is, further, a ritual garment, part of the Benedictine habit. It confers on Leoba the power and authority that devolves from Boniface's office, as abbot and as bishop. It is interesting, though not surprising, that after the death of Boniface and Leoba, the monks of Fulda refuse to honor the martry's request for their burial. Rudolf records that they "were afraid to open the holy tomb of the blessed martyr" (#21) and so buried her elsewhere.[35] But Rudolf attributes a posthumous miracle that takes place in the Fulda

[34] "Commendavit autem eam Lul episcopo et senioribus monachorum supra-dicti monasterii qui aderant, monens eos, ut cum honore et reverentia curam eius agerent, suaeque voluntatis esse affirmans, ut post obitum eius corpus illius ad ossa sua in eodem sepulchro poneretur, quatenus pariter diem resurrectionis exspectar-ent qui pari voto ac studio in vita sua Christo servierant. Quibus dictis, dedit ei cu-cullam suam. . . ." Waitz, 129, ll. 20–24.

[35] Today a museum in Fulda, the Dom Museum, is dedicated to the work of the Bonifatian mission and in one room there is an elaborate gold altarpiece that serves as a frame and display-case for the relics of the various missionaries. Surprisingly, St. Leoba is not among them. In 1999, her head was located in a locked closet of the museum, and the women of Fulda brought organized pressure on the city officials to have her head returned to the church in which the rest of her relics were placed, Michaelskirche, in a suburb of Fulda. She was brought there in the autumn of 1999 in a procession led by the women. "Plus ça change. . . ."

chapel to both saints. He editorializes that, "although not in one tomb, nevertheless . . . with the same piety with which they were accustomed to come to [someone's] assistance when they lived together in the flesh . . . they do not cease to support those seeking their intercession."[36] The monks of Fulda did not share their founder's appreciation for Leoba's partnership, but Rudolf does. He believes that their partnership is divinely confirmed by the miracle that was always, for Rudolf and early medieval theologians as a whole, the authenticating sign of true holiness and effective ministry.

Leoba's symbolic location in the bishop's home and Boniface's concern to demonstrate her partnership with him come from the fact that she is central to his episcopal project, the evangelization of Germany.[37] Rudolf returns repeatedly to this theme in his narrative. She has been chosen for her learning and she exercises, throughout her life, the ministry of teaching. He describes in great detail her intellectual formation as a youth and her achievements in learning and wisdom when she is working in Germany. Rudolf portrays her learning as the reason why Boniface chooses her for the task. Indeed, he repeats several times that it was her learning and devout life that made her fit for participation in the mission to Germany, rather than her kinship with Boniface. His insistence on this point suggests the possibility that her inclusion in the mission could be misinterpreted; her supportive presence in Boniface's life, the support only a kinswoman could offer, was important, but it was second to her intellectual gifts.

When Rudolf describes Leoba's function as teacher, he uses official, even canonical, terms to identify her position. He describes her as having

[36] "Qui, licet non in uno sepulchro, uno tamen loco quiescentes, eadem pietate, qua dum pariter in carne vixerunt miseris subvenire solebant, nunc in caelesti claritate cum Christo manentes, eorum intercessionem quaerentibus patrocinari non cessant." Waitz, 131, ll. 18–20.

[37] It is interesting to note that at the first session of the Second Vatican Council Marie-Dominique Chenu described the absence of an evangelical perspective in the preparatory schemata on the Church and what he regarded as an overemphasis on sacraments. In a letter to Mgr. Ancel of September 29, 1962, he wrote, "La transmission de la foi, le témoignage authentique de la Parole de Dieu, est la première fonction de l'Église, soit en corps, soit en hiérarchie sacrée." Cited in Chenu, *Notes quotidiennes au Concile*, ed. Alberto Mellone (Paris: Éditions du Cerf, 1995) 197, n. 1.

been placed above others "by the order of the office of teacher, *(ordine magisterii ceteris esset praelata)*" (#11). We may note here the use of the technical terms "order" and "office," although we cannot be sure of exactly what these terms meant to Rudolf. We do know that the ministry of prophecy, included in the Pauline list of ecclesiastical charisms, had come over time to include those who expounded the mysteries of scripture to the faithful. Others besides Rudolf and Maurus recognize Leoba's teaching as official and trustworthy. Rudolf notes that bishops consulted her about pastoral theology contained in the scriptures and "often" sought her counsel regarding the management of "ecclesiastical institutions."[38]

We do not have evidence of a liturgical consecration for the office of teacher at this place and time, but perhaps Rudolf suggests that there is one; the words with which he describes her character echo the words of the diaconate ordination. "Believe what you read, preach what you believe, practice what you preach." Having noted how her teaching office elevates her, Rudolf says that nonetheless she expressed both her humility and her appreciation of what this office entailed because "she believed in her heart, spoke with her voice and showed in her appearance that she wished to be last."[39] In any event, the context of Rudolf's praise makes it clear that Leoba's vocation as teacher is treated as both "order" and "office," raising her above her peers and requiring true humility lest it corrupt her sanctity and her usefulness. In this passage, Rudolf says much both about Leoba and about clerical office.

Word and Sacrament in the Mission Church

Because of Leoba's vocation as teacher, Rudolf's ecclesiology highlights the proclamation of the Word. Yet it is surprising and, indeed, problematic on several counts that there is so little evidence of sacramental activity in Rudolf's life of Leoba. First, the goal of evangelization is the full incorporation of new peoples into the life of the Church, which is accomplished only through baptism and the celebration of the Eu-

---

[38] See n. 23.

[39] "Virtutem vero humilitatis tanto studio custodivit, ut, cum merito sanctitatis et ordine magisterii ceteris esset praelata, omnium se ultimam fore corde crederet, voce proferret et habitu demonstraret." Waitz, 126, ll. 43–45.

charist. Secondly, earlier narrative literature concerning the conversion of various Germanic peoples emphasizes the moment of baptism as the turning point in the life of the individual, the Church, and the nation. Thus, Gregory of Tours, in his story of the conversion of Clovis, presents what will become a paradigmatic pattern for understanding the mission to the European Germanic tribes. In Gregory's story, the king or prince, in this case Clovis, repeats the pattern of Constantine: he is converted, though reluctantly, by a military victory, baptized by a bishop and, along with him, the conversion of the whole people is accomplished in principle if not yet in fact.[40] In direct contrast to the practice of the first four centuries, when individual baptisms followed an intensive and scripture-centered process of personal catechesis, the baptism of Clovis is the conversion of a whole nation ("gens") somehow contained within the person of the leader.[41] "King Clovis confessed his belief in God Almighty, three in one. He was baptized in the name of the Father, the Son, and the Holy Ghost, and marked in holy chrism, with the sign of the Cross of Christ. More than three thousand of his army were baptized at the same time."[42] For Clovis and his nation, as well as in many examples that followed, catechesis would come after baptism and would not always reach down to the lower strata of society.

Bede, of course, presents a somewhat different picture. There are no political or military miracles involved and the leaders of the various nations of Britain are often more cautious about speaking for all the people than Clovis seems to have been. Many of the kings whose stories Bede tells respond as does the first, King Ethelbert of Kent. "Your words and promises are fair indeed; but they are new and uncertain and I cannot accept them and abandon the age-old beliefs I have held together with the whole English nation," the king says. He then offers them the time and material support they will need to preach "and win any people

---

[40] The inadequacy of such "evangelization" is made clear by the continuing influence of pagan ideology and rites in the Germanic kingdoms. See Levison, 47–48.

[41] This pattern of the nation following the religion of the leader has clear echoes as late as the Peace of Utrecht. The principle "cujus regio, cujus religio" was finally able to bring an end to the wars of religion.

[42] Gregory of Tours, *History of the Franks* II, 31, trans. Lewis Thorpe (London: Penguin Books, 1974) 144.

[they] can to [their] religion."[43] Here the tradition of evangelization is much more continuous with ancient practice; catechesis first, individuals must answer for themselves, and miracles will confirm faith more often than provoke it. But Bede does tell the stories of the baptisms and he, too, records them as significant turning points for all concerned. I have both argued and assumed above that the mission of Boniface was greatly influenced by the Anglo-Saxon interpretations of Church traditions and his emphasis on conversion through education falls well in line with Bede's stories. But if I am correct in understanding the text of Leoba's life as an ecclesiology, we must account for the absence of any mention of baptism and Eucharist. Part of the answer, to be sure, lies in the person of Leoba herself as the center of the narrative.

As a woman, Leoba's involvement in the official liturgy of the Church would be circumscribed. Or so we assume. The Anglian monastery from which Leoba comes, was, like other double monasteries, linked to a house for monks whose services were utilized "to perform the offices of the Masses."[44] There is evidence, however, that the office of deacon, with liturgical duties, continued to be debated throughout the early Middle Ages and Venantius Fortunatus affirms that Radegunde, the subject of the last chapter in this book, was made a deacon as late as the seventh century.[45] In a thorough study of the medieval uses of the word "ordination," Gary Macy has found references to the formal and ritual consecration of deaconesses in a number of medieval manuscripts up to the twelfth century. He has found that the word might indicate the wife of a deacon or "a liturgically functioning deaconess whose exact role in the Church was unclear."[46] Under the Carolingian reform, bishops continually attempted to control women's exercise of liturgical and pastroal roles, and succeeded in restricting their activities within their

---

[43] Bede, *The Ecclesiastical History,* I, 25, 70.

[44] "ad agenda missarum official," Waitz, 123, l. 9. A similar reference is made in #21. When Leoba is dying she sends for a priest from her homeland who gives her the Eucharist as viaticum, Ibid., 130, l. 18.

[45] Suzanne Wemple, *Women in Frankish Society* (Philadelphia: University of Pennsylvania Press, 1981) 142.

[46] "The Ordination of Women in the Early Middle Ages," *TS* 61(2000) 481–507. We must remember however that ministerial language does not become fixed until the twelfth century and afterwards.

own cloisters. It is precisely in that context that we find subtle textual suggestions about Leoba's role in liturgical activities.

Certain monastic tasks contained liturgical resonance and suggest more permeable borders between monastic duties and sacramental liturgy than would later be common. Benedictine monasticism required careful attention to the duties of hospitality and providing food for guests was long connected in Christian thinking to the deacon's service at the Eucharistic table. We see such a connection in Rudolf's text. In a description of her many virtues, Rudolf writes that Leoba "kept hospitality with particular observation; for to all without any exception of person she offered a home, and as superior, though fasting, she produced a banquet. She washed the feet of everyone with her own hands as the guard and minister of the lord's institution."[47]

Here Rudolf is clearly describing Leoba in her abbatial duties to guests, enacting the Benedictine rule of hospitality. But in his references to "banquet," to the washing of the feet and to Leoba as a "minister of the lord's institution" the overtones of eucharistic practice are unmistakable. We should also remember that the ritual of the washing of the feet was long considered a sacrament and, indeed, it fits the definition of sacrament rather remarkably.[48] At the very least, Rudolf recalls here the theological link between hospitality and the Eucharist. He might be suggesting something more, although the evidence is tenuous.

In one of the miracle stories that Rudolf gives, we actually see Leoba functioning in a ritual setting. When the community has become ritually unclean through the presence of a murderer within it, Leoba "ordered everyone to enter the oratory and to stand with arms outstretched in the manner of a cross . . . . Then they went around the monastery chanting prayers and holding the cross raised up on high, invoking divine mercy

---

[47] "Hospitalitatem autem peculiari observatione tenuit; omnibus enim sine ulla exceptione personae domum praebuit et convivium ieiuna mater exhibit, pedes omnibus manibus suis lavit dominicae institutionis custos et ministra," Ibid., 126, ll. 55–57.

[48] "An outward sign instituted by Christ to give grace" is the definition given by Peter Lombard in the early twelfth century. Christ's intentional institution of the washing of the feet in John 13:1-17 is more clearly attested to than some other rituals considered sacramental.

for their purification."[49] Here is a ritual purification involving procession, prayers, gestures, an encircling of the church and the symbol of the cross—all of them liturgical elements. Leoba orders the rite and leads it; she effects a confession from the guilty party, the exoneration of the innocent and the reestablishment of the community's integrity. The format of the rite here suggests the urban rituals of the Great Litany, important in both Rome and Constantinople in the seventh and eighth centuries. The context and the outcome of the ritual suggest penitential judgment such as that found also in Rome's rogation and ember day liturgies. Though not easily identified with any specific sacramental ritual common to the period, it has strong sacramental characteristics and Leoba is the minister in this formal liturgical rite.

The connection of this ritual to an event identified as miraculous leads to another line of reflection. Is it possible to consider the miracles themselves as having a sacramental character? The very suggestion of this, of course, sounds serious alarm bells in modern readers. Since the Enlightenment, Roman Catholic theology has taken great pains to position miracles and sacraments at opposite poles of the spectrum of ritual action and with excellent reason. Within the context of a scientific worldview, blurring the lines between them led to a magical view of the sacraments that vitiated their human and ecclesiological meaning. But we must read these early texts in their own pre-scientific context and remember, first, the fluid nature of the language and thought about sacraments in the early medieval Church. It is not until the early twelfth century, in the cathedral schools and with the growing systematization of canon law as background, that theologians begin to define what a sacrament is and to limit the sacramental identification to specific liturgical rites. Second, we must remember that the miracles of Christ, recorded in the gospels, were often presented as prototypes of the sacraments by patristic commentators. Within the Gospels, the miraculous feedings of the multitudes were described in Eucharist terms and the

[49] "Quo audito, mater venerabilis de eius puritate iam secura, praecepit omnibus oratorium ingredi, et extensis in cruces modum brachiis stare, quoadusque singulae psalterium totum ex ordine psallendo complerent; et deinde per tres vices in die, hoc est hora tertia, sexta et nona, vexillo cruces elato, cum laetaniis monasterium circuire et pro purgatione sua divinam misericordiam invocare," Waitz, 127, ll. 30–34.

healing of the paralytic in Mark 3 was understood as authenticating the power of Jesus to forgive sin. Early in the development of the Roman lectionary system, certain Johannine miracles (the woman at the well, the healing of the man born blind and the raising of Lazarus) were designated as types of baptism and read during the time of preparation for that sacrament. Patristic exegetes often gave sacramental significance to the miracles of Jesus and thus it was possible for later writers to present the miracles of saints in quasi-sacramental language.

We can also find a strong similarity in the ways in which medieval theologians describe both miracles and sacraments. The medieval understanding of both was rooted in the thought of Augustine.[50] Augustine argues that the whole created universe is a single great miracle containing the seeds of all other potential miracles. For Augustine, what distinguishes miracles (as we identify them) from the other wonders of God's creation is their purpose: to create in rational creature the attitudes proper to an obedient creature and a believer. Miracles are thus propaedeutic to faith. They are phenomena within the natural order that point to the reality of the mystery beyond the natural order but revealed within it. Similarly, Augustine teaches that a sacrament is a "sacred sign" and "the visible form of an invisible thing."[51] In Chapter III of Book IV of *The Sentences,* Peter Lombard cites him to the effect that "a sign is something beyond the appearance which it presses on the sense, for it makes something else enter thought."[52] Here Lombard emphasizes the characteristic by which a sacrament captures the attention of the recipient or spectator and points it to the meaning beyond itself. Like a miracle, the sacrament appeals to the human need for external stimuli, for some event that removes the spiritual blindfold custom creates. Like

---

[50] In *De Genesi ad Litteram, De Trinitate, De Utilitate Credendi,* and *De Civitate Dei.* See Benedicta Ward, *Miracles and the Medieval Mind* (Philadelphia: University of Pennsylvania Press, 1987) 3–4.

[51] Cited in Peter Lombard, *The Sentences,* bk. V in *A Scholastic Miscellany: Anselm to Ockham,* ed. Eugene R. Fairweather (Philadelphia: The Westminster Press, 1956) 338–39. That Lombard's work on sacraments is virtually a catena of Augustine's citations and a gloss upon them indicates the centrality of Augustine's thought in the tradition of sacramental theology.

[52] Ibid., 358.

a miracle, a sacrament uses the events and elements of the natural and sensual world to point to something beyond itself, something that one can only apprehend by reason illuminated by faith.

Further, speaking in his own name but as a gloss on Augustine, the Lombard notes that sacraments are signs "of the grace of God and a form of invisible grace, so that it bears its image and exists as its cause" (ch. IV).[53] This is the aspect of sacrament which makes it more than instructional, but truly causal, an instance of intense divine presence which brings about the necessary healing and salvation. Because it is causal, the sacramental effect is always consonant with the specific ritual or sign that effects it.

The miracles that Rudolf narrates fit well into medieval descriptions of both miracles and sacraments. If we think of the sacraments as actions embodying the saving presence of Christ within the community of faith, it is not difficult to extend this notion to the miracles presented by Rudolf. In each case, there are specific actions performed by someone acting in the name of the Church and out of the fullness of the Church's faith. Though Leoba is not a cleric, she has been designated as an official leader in the Church at Fulda and Boniface has invested her with his own authority. Furthermore, when she acts as abbess (as she does in each of these miracles), she is acting in an official capacity and representing the Church, not just herself. The actions she performs prepare the minds of those who are present to receive appropriate instruction. The sign or *virtus* that is done indicates the precise nature of the teaching and is, in itself, instructional. It both confirms the teaching and confirms the presence of God acting within the teacher. Finally, the sign or wonder brings about what it signifies, a judgment and an act of salvation or healing.

Rudolf narrates several such miracles attributed to Leoba when she is alive. In the first, the nuns are maliciously accused of infanticide and, even more importantly, of polluting the community's water source by placing a dead infant within the local stream. The stream is the community's water source; contaminating it puts the entire community at risk and Rudolf is clear about the gradations of evil perpetrated. "[C]learly

---

[53] Ibid., 339.

adding evil to evil, . . . she joined murder to unchastity and contamination of water to murder."[54] The whole village rises up in anger and dismay, they accuse the nuns of sinful behavior at odds with their vows and an attack against the community. The death of the baby becomes an occasion for rejecting, not only the presence of a sinful nun, but also Christ and the faith the nuns have preached. After making prudent investigation of the facts, Leoba petitions for divine judgment by enacting the cleansing ritual described above. When the entire community, having completed the ritual, gathers in the Church, Leoba prays, "Lord Jesus Christ, king of virgins, lover of integrity, invincible God, show your virtue and free us from this infamy, because the reproaches of those blaming you have fallen upon us."[55] Then the true sinner confesses and "with one voice the merit of the virgin Leoba and the power of Christ the savior was proclaimed by all in common."

In this story, Christ the judge is also Christ, the Savior. To experience the judgment of Christ in time (rather than at the end of time) is to experience the opportunity for salvation by Christ. Such an opportunity is, ordinarily, offered through the tribunal of penance and, extraordinarily, through a miracle such as this one. The miracle is clearly the action of the saving Christ, made visible through the ritual and faith of the community assembled and there are references to baptism throughout. Rudolf notes that this was not the first miracle in Leoba's life but it "was the first in Germany and was so celebrated because it was public."[56] He does not narrate this as *the* turning point in the life of the German Christian community, but it is a great and "public sign" and a significant moment in that story.

Rudolf narrates two other miracles in quick succession; both show Leoba confronting fierce natural forces. In the first, she confronts a fire

[54] "malis videlicet mala adiciens; nam stupro homicidium et aquae contaminationem coniunxit homicidio," Waitz, 127, ll. 11–12.

[55] "Domine Ihesu Christe, rex virginum, integritatis amator, invictissime Deus, ostende virtutem tuam et libera nos ab hac infamia, quia inproperia inproperantium tibi ceciderunt super nos," Ibid., ll. 37–39.

[56] "Plura quidem signa per famulam suam Deus ante iam fecerat, sed eorum notitiam secreti obumbratio suppressit, hoc autem in Germania primum et ideo celebre, quia publicum fuit," Ibid., ll. 45–47.

that begins accidentally but soon, "carried by driving gusts of wind"[57] threatens the entire village and monastery. In the second, it is "a raging storm and a very great disturbance of the weather"[58] from which she is required to protect the nuns and villagers. In each case, the threat is described in terms that suggest the darkness of evil. The fire "threatens" everyone "with destruction," there is "a confused clamor" when the people recognize "the whole destructive force of the fires . . . ." Even more explicitly, the storm is described as a supra-natural evil: fog makes the day into night, the presence of death is within the storm and the words "darkness," "rage," "invasion," and the like are repeated in a crescendo of danger. The people are filled with "terror" and "awaited the terrible judgment of God."

In each case, Leoba responds to the threat with actions that echo elements of baptism. Against the fire, she sprinkles salt into the monastery's well water and it douses the flames. Against the storm, as she is assembled with the whole community in the church, "she arose from her prayer and, throwing aside the cape in which she was dressed as if she were called to a death struggle, she confidently opened the doors of the church. She stood on the threshold, made the sign of the holy cross, put forth the name of the Greatest Majesty against the raging storm. With her hands stretched out to heaven, she invoked the mercy of Christ three times in a shout . . . and prayed that He, merciful, would quickly present for His people."[59] The salt and water of the fire miracle are clear echoes of baptism and in the miraculous calming of the storm, we see the stripping of garments, the signing with the cross and the three-fold shout. All of these suggest moments in the ancient ritual of the great baptismal Easter Vigil. Leoba stands at the church door; if the church were oriented in the Roman manner, she is facing west, in the direction of evil, the position often assumed by catechumens when they

---

[57] Ibid., l. 48–128, l. 6.

[58] Ibid., 128, ll. 7–30.

[59] "Ad hanc vocem illa ab oratione surrexit, et quasi ad colluctationem vocaretur, sanctae crucis edito, furenti tempestati nomen Summae Maiestatis opposuit, extensisque manibus in caelum, terno clamore Christi clementiam invocavit et per intercessionem ac merita sanctae Mariae virginis propitium eum populo suo velociter adesse precabatur," Ibid., ll. 22–26.

renounced Satan three times before turning eastward to pronounce their triple acceptance of Christ.

These two miracles, as well as the miracle of judgment on infanticide that precedes them, are exorcisms as well as nature miracles; they recall the importance of the miracles of exorcism in the Gospels and the centrality of exorcisms in the liturgy of baptism. In a mission context, the reality of the evil that must be renounced in commitment to Christ is made visible in these miracles; it is a dynamic patterned on the traditional Christian understanding of baptism. After her death, Leoba continues to do miracles through the presence of her relics in the church at Fulda. Rudolf narrates two; they are both healing miracles in which the sickness is clearly identified as the consequence of sin. These miracles of physical healing and the forgiveness of sin not only echo the sacrament of reconciliation, but are a reminder of how often, in the Gospels, the miracles of Jesus had also accomplished both kinds of cure. The nexus between healing and forgiveness also indicates a ninth-century understanding of healings and anointing before they disappear into the one sacrament of extreme unction.

I do not mean for a moment to suggest that the local church of southern Germany did not follow the usual practice of liturgical sacraments or that Rudolf does not recognize the importance and distinctiveness of the latter. But I do want to suggest that in the early Germanic churches, the theological understanding of sacraments was not all that distinct from the understanding of miracles. Both involved ritual actions and symbolic objects; both were patterned on gospel events and stories but expressed in the local idiom; both were occasioned by the specific needs of the people assembled. Miracles and sacraments alike were occasions for the manifestation of the saving and powerful presence of Christ in the local community. The dynamic, subtle, ever-changing interplay between word and sacrament that constitutes the mystery of Church in every age can be seen in Rudolf's presentation of a similar matrix of word and miracle in the life of Leoba. Guided by the story he tells of a woman whose liturgical responsibilities, if any, are difficult to ascertain, he focuses on her extraordinarily important role in the ministry of the word and the way in which that ministry was completed and confirmed in the power of Christ present in miracle.

Christology and Anthropology for a Church in Mission

Within the Christian tradition Christology and anthropology are integral to ecclesiology and are mutually informative each of the other. The Church's self-understanding is dependent on the way it understands Christ in his fullness, the Christ of history and the Christ of faith. Similarly, how the Church understands and proclaims Christ, the second person of the Trinity made flesh, will be conditioned by, and will further shape, how human nature is understood. Therefore, to fully understand the ecclesiology of Rudolf's life of Leoba, we must also investigate the Christology and anthropology within the text. It is axiomatic that the Christology and anthropology of the ninth century depended on the patristic legacy. But the latter was never fully systematized; rather it came down to early medieval theologians in a fragmentary form within the context of biblical exegesis. The starting point of patristic Christology was always soteriology and what early medieval theologians inherited from the fathers was a series of soteriological models, based on biblical texts.[60]

These models include the pedagogical model of salvation and the recapitulation model, both of which are to be found in Rudolf's narrative. In the pedagogical model, Christ is described as other than the Christian, the one who reveals the Godhead and teaches the way of salvation by how he lives and dies. This is the Christ with whom Christians enter into relationship, the Christ who is Lord and Savior, the one mediator between God and those who are saved. In the recapitulation model, Christ is understood as one with the community of the baptized; he is the head of his body, which is the Church. Incorporated into Christ, the Christian community continues the saving presence of Christ in history and thus makes it possible for those of later generations to meet Christ and be saved by him. Both of these Christological models, which are neither mutually exclusive nor sufficient unto themselves, are to be found in Rudolf's text.

1. Christ as Lord and Examplar

References to Christ are relatively sparse within the life of Leoba (some sixteen in all). Not surprisingly, a number of these refer to the

---

[60] See Joseph A. Mitros, "Patristic Views of Christ's Salvific Work," *Thought* 42, 166 (Autumn, 1967) 415–47. This is a very helpful, though not recent, essay. It is faithful to the patristic texts and its schematization provides insight into medieval usage.

place Christ holds in the life of those dedicated to him, a Christ in personal relationship with those who love and serve him. In his dedication, for example, Rudolf calls Hadamotam, the nun to whom he sends the text, "a devout virgin **of Christ**" who assists her with his grace and Christ's **"consort"** ("Preamble," emphasis mine). He prays to Christ as Leoba's bridegroom, "the Lord God and our savior," who is the source of Leoba's courage. The metaphors of bridegroom and consort convey, on the one hand, the intimacy of the relationship between Christ and the believer and, on the other, a relationship of power and partnership. The consort shared the responsibility and power of dominion with an earthly king; the suggestion is that intimate relationship with Christ bestows on the believer a share, a partnership, in Christ's power to save. Christ empowers because he is the Lord God; he gives "assisting grace" to Hadamotam and courage to Leoba. Union with Christ becomes the ground of all other relationship between Christians; here, Hadamotam is a "virgin **of Christ**" and later in the same section Rudolf will describe Tetta as Leoba's "mother **in Christ**."[61]

The personal relationship of which Rudolf speaks is not individualistic or exclusive; to enter into relationship with Christ is to be at once in relationship with all others who also believe. This is the Christ who is the foundation of the Church, the Christ into whose one body all are baptized (a pervasive Pauline image); ecclesiastical relationships, rooted in Christ, are therefore always personal and not just institutional. Some contemporary scholars have noted the intimacy and mutuality that marked the network of relationships between all of the Anglo-Saxon missionaries to Germany.

These scholars have opined that the importance of kinship bonds in Anglo-Saxon culture explains the language and affectivity of their correspondence.[62] If so, the usage of Anglo-Saxon culture was quite consonant

---

[61] See also #12, where Leoba is called "virgin of Christ."

[62] See Catherine Wybourne, "Leoba: A Study in Humanity and Holiness" in *Medieval Women Monastics*, ed. Miriam Schmitt and Linda Kulzer (Collegeville: Liturgical Press, 1996) 81–96, and Deborah Harmeling, "Tetta, 'Noble in Conduct,' and Thecla, 'Shining Like a Light in a Dark Place,'" Ibid., 99–114. The latter author cites Stephanie Hollis, *Anglo-Saxon Women and the Church* (Woodbridge: The Boydell Press, 1992).

with the language of the Pauline epistles where familial language is used
for church relationships and affectionate intimacy marks Paul's own address to his correspondents. Even within this communitarian understanding of Christian life, however, the individual relationship with Christ
remains central, important and capable of varying degrees of intensity. In
#7, Rudolf describes Leoba as one who is "burning with desire for Christ"
and notes, in #11, that Christ possesses her heart. The Christ who is the
foundation of the Church and the ground of all its relationships is the
same Christ who is the object of mystical love and desire. Moving as he
does from the individual to the communal, Rudolf consistently emphasizes the deeply and essentially relational character of the Church.

He maintains this emphasis, even when he depicts Christ as the
powerful lord and savior who is the object of intercessory prayer and
the source of saving power. This dimension of Rudolf's Christology is
most visible in the miracles that he narrates and interprets. In the story
Rudolf tells about Tetta, the abbess who trained Leoba for her life and
mission, Tetta invokes Christ in order to bring about reconciliation between her nuns and a sister who has died while in a state of enmity with
the community. Having reminded the community that Christian perfection required them to love their enemies and that their own hope of
forgiveness depended on their willingness to forgive, Tetta orders them
to fast and then to gather in the church for intercessory litanies. There
she "invok[es] the name of the Savior and the help of his saints" (4).
Christ is the intercessor, the one mediator between God and the community, but it is the whole Christ, head and members, who is active, the
Lord who is helped by his companion saints.

Although in this story, it is the power of Christ that is important, the
relational dimension of the Christ of faith is integral to that power. After
the Resurrection, Christ cannot be separated from those who are incorporated into him; from this central Christian truth flows the power of
the saints. In the miracle occasioned by the dead infant described above,
we see a similar understanding of Christ. After she has carried the cross
in procession around the monastery, Leoba addresses Christ in prayer.
"Lord Jesus Christ, king of virgins, lover of integrity, invincible God,
show your virtue and free us from this infamy, because the reproaches of
those blaming you have fallen upon us." Here Christ is invoked as judge
and "invincible God," but he is also the one who lives in relationship with

those who believe in him, the "king of [these] virgins." As judge, he is neither vengeful nor arbitrary, but a "lover of integrity."

Again, Christ is seen as the head of a community of faith, so much so that those who would wage war against him battle with those who love him. Christ and this community are one. In all of these miracles, a completely traditional and orthodox Christology is manifest. Christ is the one true God with the power to know all things and to do all things. He is the object of prayer; he is judge and savior; he is exemplar. But he is also eternally united to, and present in, the community of faith, acting in concert with Mary and all the saints and through their intercession and that of the holy ones on earth (like Leoba and Tetta).

2. Christ Present in His Saints

A second dimension of Rudolf's Christology emphasizes the humanity and immanence of Christ rather than his divinity and transcendence. It flows from and is dependent upon Rudolf's understanding that Christ now is to be identified with the community of those incorporated into him. As the son of God assumed a complete human nature without destroying it, so does the grace of God, through baptism into Christ, transform human persons into other Christs while leaving their own humanity intact. Thus Christ continues to act in and for the community of faith through those whom he calls to be his saints.

Scholars have long noted the fundamental patterns in hagiographical texts: stories are repeated with only the names of the major actors changed, miracles are suspiciously repetitive, and catalogs of virtues move from one saint to another. Scholars have noted, as does Pauline Head in specific reference to the text of Leoba's life, "[s]uch events come from a common stock of material."[63] But the ultimate source of this "common stock" is clearly the scriptural narratives that served also as model of the *vita sanctorum*.[64] In a study of the process by which oral traditions became written hagiography, Thomas Heffernan, makes two points that are pertinent to

---

[63] "'Integritas' in Rudolf of Fulda's *Vita Leobae Abbatissae*," *Parergon* New Series 13, 1 (July, 1995) 40.

[64] See, in this regard, John A. Alford, "The Scriptural Self," in *The Bible in the Middle Ages: Its Influence on Literature and Art*, ed. Bernard S. Levy (Binghamton, N.Y.: Medieval & Renaissance Texts & Studies, 1992) 3–4.

this study.[65] In regard to an author's use of the "common stock" of saintly material, Heffernan notes that the narrator is not exactly trying to create "generic saint" or to imply that to have seen one saint was to have seen them all! Rather the author is creating exemplary models, "by means of rhetorically sophisticated and avowedly mimetic reminiscences of the life of Christ."[66] In other words, the narrator is presenting the saint as Christ himself, living in a new situation and a new context, a profoundly Christological principle. Indeed, Heffernan describes the constraints that guide the narrator's work in clearly Christological language. "The subject must be made to appear fully human while that which is being written must confirm and celebrate his or her 'otherness.'" Intentionally or not, Heffernan also adverts to the Christology that grounds the authorial process. Later saints can be described in stories and phrases borrowed from the Gospels because, theologically understood, the saints are Christ, members of his body and the contemporary *loci* of his saving presence, an insight completely consistent with traditional theology.

The Pauline Epistles are foundational to this theology. In 1 Corinthians, *inter alia,* Paul identifies the Christian as Christ himself when discussing ritual prostitution. "Do you not know that your bodies are limbs and organs of Christ?" (6:15a). Paul consistently understands himself as Christ ("Imitate me as I imitate Christ") and he consistently speaks of baptism as an *incorporation into Christ*. This theme can be found in Luke's *Acts of the Apostles* as well, especially in the early chapters where Peter performs miracles that echo those of Christ. Tertullian spoke of "the Christian as another Christ," and in one of the earliest pieces of hagiographical literature Athanasius presents Antony the hermit as Christ, especially in the scene in which Antony emerges from the cave. The cult of the saints begins with the martyrs, because they most perfectly replicated the historical life of Christ giving themselves "even unto death."[67] And Peter Brown's analysis of the role of the "holy man"

---

[65] *Sacred Biography* (New York & Oxford: Oxford University Press, 1988) 26.

[66] Heffernan, 30.

[67] Elizabeth Johnson also points to the christological significance of the martyrs in *Friends of God and Prophets* (Ottawa: Novalis, 1998) 73. Her emphasis throughout, however, is on the kind of "communio" that bound all believers together, in Christ rather than on the one who is officially or spontaneously named another Christ.

in late antique society shows that this early saintly figure continues to be a healing and reconciling presence in the manner of Christ.[68] Thus, the Resurrected Christ, living forever in the glory of the Father, continues his historical existence in another person, who has been incorporated into him in baptism; thus he extends his salvific work to other times and places. The historical and concrete life and work of Leoba, therefore, is an important dimension of the Christology of Rudolf's text.

Rudolf identifies Leoba as another Christ in several ways. Her prophetic status is signified by the two dreams that foretell her birth and her vocation. Like Jesus (and the prophets before him, especially Samuel), Leoba is set aside for God's purposes from the womb. Like Christ and in his name, she works miracles. In one of several catalogs of her virtues (that rhetorical mainstay of hagiography), Rudolf notes that "to all who obeyed her in word and manner of life, she appeared **as a form of salvation**" (#11, emphasis mine). As Paul instructed, Leoba has so thoroughly "put on the mind of Christ" that she becomes, like Christ, an experience of salvation for those who listen and learn. But most of all, she is identified with Jesus, the teacher. Christ, the Teacher, was a perennial and important title in the developing Christology and soteriology of the patristic period. It is a primary dimension of Matthew's portrait of Christ and Clement of Alexandria also made Christ's role as teacher the foundation of his Christology in *Paedagogus* written very early in the third century. This notion remained an essential dimension of christological thought to both the Antiochene and Alexandrian schools and endured throughout the patristic period in theology and preaching. In emphasizing Leoba's teaching vocation as the formative center of her life and in describing the way in which her teaching is by both instruction and example, Rudolf tells her story as that of another Christ.

Like Jesus, Leoba teaches a **living word of God,** that is, she explains the scriptures, but even more, she exemplifies them. Rudolf tells us that in setting up his missionary team, Boniface sought evangelists "suitable for preaching the living word by their merit and probity of character" (#9). Leoba does not disappoint Boniface's expectations. Rudolf shows

---

[68] Peter Brown, "The Rise and Function of the Holy Man in Late Antiquity," in *Society and the Holy in Late Antiquity* (Oxford and Los Angeles: University of California Press, 1982) 103–52.

that in her work and in her person, Jesus the teacher is present in Leoba, explaining the scriptures as he did throughout the public life, exemplifying the scriptures by her extraordinary virtues, and, when the situation warrants, making the power of Christ's Word and Christ as Word effective in miraculous acts of salvation. Because Leoba is, as all other Christians, another Christ, the discussion of her humanity is an exploration of the ideal of human nature. In the christological tradition of the Church, Christ does not only reveal who God is for us; he also reveals what it means to be fully and completely human. Therefore the Christology of Rudolf's text tells us something of his own anthropology, specifically the relationship between nature and grace.

3. Anthropology

Rudolf's anthropology is best understood under the theme of nature and grace. He exposes the intimate interaction between nature and grace in a number of significant ways. He stresses wisdom as the hallmark of Leoba's life and accomplishments. He also highlights the way in which Leoba and her teachers act always according to reason, that natural human gift that is, in Christian anthropology, the foundation of all moral action and, indeed, of all holiness. Finally, he demonstrates how Leoba's holiness is not an immoderate pursuit of all virtues, willy-nilly, but is rather the result of moderation (that quality dear to Aristotle) and the shaping of her life according to the demands of her vocation.

The theme of wisdom, as it is developed in this text, demonstrates the complete interdependence of nature and grace. Wisdom is grace, freely given by God. At the same time, it comes as a gift to those who prepare for it, principally through study, learning and the acquisition of appropriate virtues. So does Augustine speak of it in one of his episcopal sermons[69] and in his commentary on the Sermon on the Mount.[70] In the commentary, Augustine parallels the eight beatitudes and the seven gifts of the Holy Spirit and proposes that the Beatitudes describe the efforts of the human person freely to grow in virtue while the gifts of the Holy Spirit (Isa 11:2f.) describe the operation of the Holy Spirit (grace). For

---

[69] Augustine, "Sermo," 347, *PL* 139, cols. 1524ff.

[70] Augustine, *The Lord's Sermon on the Mount, Ancient Christian Writers,* 5 trans. John J. Jepson (Westminster, Md.: Newman Press, 1956).

Augustine, the beatitudes about the meek and those who mourn describe the soul engaged in the study of the Holy Scripture through which she arrives at the higher stages of Christian life[71] and wisdom is the culminating gift that crowns academic study and confers perfect peace. Wisdom is solid intellectual knowledge honed by discipline and virtue until it culminates into an almost instinctive understanding of how to act under all conditions. It is spiritual and theocentric: Christ is the incarnate wisdom of God and his saints share in that wisdom, acting consistently according to the divine will and judgment. It is practical and humane: the "wise virgins" store up on oil and the wise provide for the present and the future. Wisdom is the crown of all the moral virtues; it subsumes prudence, justice, temperance, and fortitude and gives to all of them a particular sweetness and ease. The mutual interplay between human effort and divine grace as it flourishes in wisdom permeates Augustine's description of the Christian life and became embedded in the monastic ideals of Christian life and holiness.

Rudolf gives various catalogues of Leoba's virtues in the traditional manner, but he emphasizes throughout how the search for wisdom through intensive biblical study brought about all other virtues in her. Rudolf narrates how Leoba, like the parabolic virgins, carefully cultivated both discretion and prudence; she always considered the desired outcome of a plan of action, "lest by chance she might begin things illadvisedly and later have to regret her inability to complete them."[72] We see Leoba's wisdom in a number of different situations. Leoba acts quickly but wisely to resolve the terrors and conflicts of her local convent-village, finding the guilty pauper whose crimes have threatened the local water-supply (#12) and protecting the village from both fire (#13) and storm (#14). On one level, these are miracle stories, but they are also vignettes of Leoba's wisdom, practical and spiritual at the same time. Rudolf consistently affirms that Leoba's wisdom is valued by the powerful leaders of her own day. Although Leoba hates the courts and their feverish, noisy atmosphere, princes, nobles, and bishops sought her

[71] Jepson, 14–21.

[72] "Discretionem in omni actu ac dispositione sua magnopere servavit et rerum faciendarum finem semper adtendit, ne forte inconsulte coepta postmodum inperfectione sua paenitentiam sibi generarent," Waitz, 126, ll. 30–32.

counsel and her interpretation of the scriptures in organizing social life and "ecclesiastical institutions" (#18).

What others seek of Leoba and what Rudolf praises in her is a wisdom built on reason as its indispensable foundation. To elaborate more fully on the importance of reason in Leoba's world, Rudolf introduces his narrative by an exposition of her early formation. In fact, Rudolf spends a little over a quarter of the whole text on the monastery from which she comes and its abbess, Tetta. He discusses the structure and principles of governance on which the monastery of Wimborne was founded and gives an extended description of Leoba's early experiences there, with a special emphasis on her education. So much does Rudolf develop this material, that we must suppose it to be a kind of hermeneutic key to understanding Leoba and her work in the mission of Saxony.[73] Wimborne was an ancient royal foundation in Britain, a double monastery, ruled by the abbess, in which the monks served the clerical needs of the nuns. Rudolf's description stresses the rational principles upon which Wimborne was founded and administered, an exposition of the importance of reason in doing the work of God. The walls of the monastery were "high and strong" and no expense had been spared on its **"rational arrangement"**[74] of buildings, material and financial resources. The discipline that separated the sexes and the enclosure of the women was strictly enforced but exceptions to enclosure were admitted when "a cause of great **reason or usefulness** arose."[75]

Rudolf stresses that the monastic institution and rule are at the service of human growth and holiness; neither human needs nor human reason are sacrificed to an arbitrary rule. Material conditions are properly provided in order that the community will have the best possible opportunity to reach holiness. The discipline of the enclosure similarly serves the women. Rudolf notes that Tetta not only keeps clerics and laymen out of the cloister, but bishops as well. This probably does not

---

[73] Some would argue that Rudolf describes the English monastery at length to stress the difference between it and Leoba's own foundation, that he wishes to support the reform movement that eliminated double monasteries. Such an interpretation does not preclude an anthropological interpretation as well.

[74] "sufficientia sumptuum rationabili dispositione procurata," Waitz, 123, l. 5.

[75] "nisi causa rationabilis vel magnae ciuislibet utilitatis existens," Ibid., l. 12.

indicate that bishops were more likely to be sexual threats than other orders of men; their specific threat was their power. Bishops were quite likely to want to meddle in the affairs of women's monasteries; where the monastery was rich and influential, bishops could use their ecclesiastical authority to exploit the community. Tetta's concern for discipline is not only, perhaps not primarily, an issue of sexual probity but a desire to maintain the autonomy and integrity of the community, to keep Wimborne a woman's place where their own purposes could be fulfilled. As is clear from the way in which Rudolf writes of Leoba's education, Wimborne founded its holiness on the pursuit of learning.

Rudolf tells the story of Leoba's early training in great detail and with a strong emphasis on the style, content and methods of monastic learning in her day and his own.[76] As Rudolf describes it, education means a combination of reading and hearing the text as well as committing it to memory. Reading and listening would have required a study of Latin grammar (since Leoba would have spoken a dialect of Anglo-Saxon), as well as the study of classical logic and rhetoric in order that she might construe the authentic religious meaning of the text. Rudolf states explicitly that she had learned grammar and the other liberal arts. Committing the text to memory had a twofold importance: it constituted the actual process of learning and it was the means by which the teaching of the text became a determining force in one's actions. Rudolf makes this latter connection quite explicit. Leoba, he says, "studied carefully lest the things she heard or read should slip from her mind; she guarded the teachings of the Lord so that the memory of them shaped the performance of her works."[77] Biblically based action was the primary goal of scriptural study; what Leoba learns in the monastery is "divine studies" (#6) and "heavenly discipline" (#7). The goal is spiritual and supernatural; the means of arriving at it are rational and practical.

---

[76] For a full description of monastic learning as understood by Rudolf and his contemporaries, see Jean LeClercq, *The Love of Learning and the Desire for God*, trans. Catharine Misrahi (New York: Fordham University Press, 1967) especially ch. 5, "Sacred Learning," 87–109.

[77] "summopere studens, ne lecta vel audita ex eius animo laberentur, sed praecepta Domini custodiens, memoriam eorum in executione operum semper habere consuevit," Waitz, 125, ll. 5–6.

Rudolf notes the balance of nature and grace in all of his descriptions of Leoba's learning and teaching. When he narrates how Leoba devoted herself to the education of others in Saxony (#11), Rudolf says that her attention to reading is marked by both "diligence" and "enthusiasm," that is, both virtue and natural inclination inform her devotion to study. Indeed, "since her reading was consistent with her natural talent, by the double blessing of nature and industry, she became most learned."[78] Here we have the clearest possible statement about the relationship of nature and grace. She pursues the study of "the Holy Fathers," canonical decrees "and the laws of the entire ecclesiastical order." In other words, she studies every aspect of learning available. But Leoba knows that learning is not wisdom; nature, no matter how finely tuned by discipline, is not grace. So Rudolf tells us that she seeks to bring knowledge to the perfection of wisdom through "a great eagerness for spiritual meditation."

Leoba's diligence in learning is both the cause and the result of her ecclesial vocation as a teacher, the source of likeness to Christ and, from all the evidence in her *vita,* her own joy and enthusiasm. She loses no opportunity to teach and images of Leoba teaching thread through Rudolf's text. So competent is she that soon her pupils are sought by other monasteries to be teachers in their turn (#11). Her success in education and the virtuous reputation of her students provoke a diabolic attack (#12). Invited by Queen Hildegarde to remain at the court as her spiritual advisor, she rejects its dangerous allures "like a cup of poison," and visits, instead, "the monastery of girls" where she continues her teaching ministry (#18). There is even the suggestion that when she visits the monastery of Fulda for prayer (a privilege granted to no other woman), she stays for a "meeting with the monks" (#19). Though teaching is not explicitly mentioned, given that her visits to Fulda were at the command of Boniface and that he himself had constituted her an official teacher, we may assume that she either taught the monks while she was there or, at the least, discussed spiritual matters to their mutual instruction. Rudolf says that she teaches virtually up to the last day of her life (#18 and 19).

Leoba understands that the vocation of teaching requires her to fit her actions to her words and so the scripture that she teaches becomes

---

[78] "consentiente cum ingenio lectione, duplicato naturae et industriae bono eruditissima redderetur," Ibid., 126, ll. 26–27.

her moral and ascetical program as well (#11). Through her commitment to teaching she learns fortitude and perseverance; by it she is "strengthened in the vigor of [her] resolution" (#11). Through her vocation as teacher she develops temperance. She was frugal in food and drink; while she graciously provided "the enjoyment of food and drink for others with the greatest kindness," she herself took most sparingly for herself (#11). With insight into the delicate mutual interaction of nature and grace, Leoba recognizes that both prayer and "diligent reading" require a humane and balanced life; she insists that proper periods of rest be observed. Rudolf quotes what seems to have been a kind of aphorism she frequently repeated: "when sleep is taken away, sense is taken away, especially for reading."[79] Asceticism is not what she is trying to promote; a learned holiness is.[80] Indeed, her asceticism was shaped by her educational commitments—she is single-minded in ordering her time for study—and not by arbitrary norms borrowed from the lives of anchorites, hermits, and those devoted to a penitential existence. She observed "due measure" in the practice of virtue and was not excessive in ascetical exercises.

Of all the other virtues that Rudolf attributes to her, he notes that she particularly cultivates humility and hospitality. Her humility is neither self-abasement nor self-hatred but rather a very specific remedy for the concrete situation in which Leoba finds herself. She is the eminent teacher of the region and a missionary from another land and culture. Anything that suggested arrogance could endanger her mission as well as threaten her own virtue. Humility is an essential safeguard for her. Her practice of hospitality is also a virtue required by her position; she keeps hospitality "without any exception of person"—an extension of her humility—and it is integral to her abbatial office, though Leoba does it with particular grace.

---

[79] "dixit enim, adempto somno sensum adimi, maxime legendi," Ibid., l. 35.

[80] Rudolf Bell, *Holy Anorexia* (Chicago and London: University of Chicago Press, 1985) argues that the self-starvation he documents begins in the thirteenth century. Caroline Bynum, *Jesus As Mother* (Berkeley: University of California Press, 1982) finds evidence in the twelfth. Both deal with women long after Leoba and, significantly, when the learning that was her source of autonomy was no longer so accessible to women.

According to Rudolf, Leoba does not do more or other than her office requires, but she does it with particular attentiveness, yet another example of the delicate balance between nature and grace. Rudolf does, of course, give the occasional purely rhetorical list of virtues, generic to hagiography and unrelated to the person of Leoba herself.[81] But overall he paints a portrait of one who is saintly because she is fully living her ecclesial vocation, shaping her character to its demands. She is not devoted to the development of virtues as such but to the search for wisdom, from which all other virtues, especially those necessary to her state in life, flow.[82]

Within the narrative that Rudolf tells, there is one story that does not make a good deal of sense unless we read it as a foil to Leoba's own holiness. It is the story of a woman in Tetta's monastery identified only as "a certain nun" who is celebrated for her "enthusiasm for discipline and observance of a stricter life;"[83] Rudolf describes her as "indiscreet" and lacking caution; she has "a stubborn heart," *(contumaci corde)* persists in rigidity, lacks mercy for others and—the final sin of the good person—she despises those who do not emulate her severity. The nun so described provides a foil to Rudolf's description of Leoba. Even in her youth at Wimborne, Leoba acknowledges the virtues of others, praising and imitating them, attentive to the demands of charity. The

---

[81] Earlier in #11 we read: "Erit enim aspectu angelica, sermone iocunda, ingenio clara, consilio magna, fide catholica, spe patientissima, karitate diffusa; et cum laetam semper faciem praeferret, numquam hilaritate nimia resolute est in risum. Maledictionem ex eius ore nullus umquam audivit, iracundiae illius sol numquam testis occubuit," Ibid., ll. 18–21. "For she was angelic in appearance, pleasing in conversation, clear in intelligence, great in counsel, orthodox in faith, most patient in hope, expansive in charity and, although she always offered a happy face, she never dissolved in laughter with too much hilarity. No one ever heard a curse from her mouth; never the setting sun a witness of her anger."

[82] On this point, I disagree strongly with Pauline Head who writes: "In keeping with hagiographical convention, the most important virtue which Leoba exemplifies is that of virginity," "'Integritas,'" 46. Though Leoba is consistently called "the virgin Leoba," Rudolf's presentation of her virtues is much more complex than that and the focus is clearly on wisdom rather than virginity.

[83] "propter disciplinae studium et artioris vitae observantiam," Waitz, 123, ll. 26–27.

result is that "all the sisters loved her with pure affection."[84] To cultivate the natural qualities that make one acceptable or attractive to others can be the necessary ground of supernatural virtue, especially for one who aspires to live in a single-gender community where jealously and competitiveness are easy traps. It is also an essential quality for the missionary and Rudolf recognizes it in the mature Leoba, at work in the mission field of Saxony. There Rudolf describes her as having "nothing of arrogance or pride" in her character; in no way domineering over others, "she showed herself to be affable and benevolent to all."[85]

Perhaps above all other ecclesial vocations, the missionary must demonstrate sensitivity to the feelings of those to whom she ministers. The conviction that one is bringing "the good news" can imbue an evangelist with feelings of superiority, a conviction that one has the right to control others and an attitude of condescension; history is replete with examples. Leoba's virtue is that she avoids all these "natural" attitudes and instead develops a manner that is "naturally" appealing and gracious. In these short, pithy descriptions, Rudolf gives us a succinct theology of virtue. Grace fulfills and transforms nature and does not substitute for it; the cultivation of a naturally attractive personality is an act of virtue, especially for the Christian in community or with a missionary vocation. The subtle interaction of nature and grace in Leoba is truly remarkable; that Rudolf recognizes it and in no way upsets the balance in the telling of her story is also to be noted. He praises no excess of virtue in her; he does not minimize the importance of her natural gifts for her own salvation and that of others. In this context, the miracles she performs, the acts of divine power that operate in and through her holy presence confirm the authenticity of the anthropology taught here. Grace does come to Leoba's human nature and, through her, to the whole community of faith within which she lives out her ministry as missionary.

Conclusion: Rudolf's Ecclesiology and the Four Marks of the Church

A theology of mission is, in itself, an ecclesiology. Christian faith is ecclesial; it is not the inchoate or unspecified belief in a deity, but a belief

---

[84] "ab universes sororibus puro diligebatur affectu," Ibid., 125, ll. 6–7.
[85] "omnibus se affabilem ac benivolam exhibuit," Ibid., 126, l. 18.

in the Father of Our Lord Jesus Christ whose earthly mission of redemption is continued by and in the community of faith that is called
Church. In undertaking to communicate the faith to those still outside
of it, therefore, the missionary acts out of specific understanding of
Church and makes the Church present as an instrument of redemption.
When Boniface chooses a "deputation" as the means of enacting the
mission and chooses particular members to participate, he is demonstrating a collegial understanding of the Church. When he invites Leoba
to be his partner in the mission and reaffirms her partnership with dramatic gestures of inclusion, he implies his openness to the role of women
as official members of that Church.

In recognizing her particular gift of learning and giving opportunities for its use, Boniface demonstrates that Christian faith is as much an
appeal to the reasoning mind as to the power of the emotions or of the
social environment. Further, he sees no difference between men and
women in their potential for a reasoned faith, for participation in a
learned Christian culture. One of the most learned persons in the mission, Leoba stands as the very witness to that understanding of faith, a
clear and conscious rejection of the ancient tradition that denied the full
expression of personhood to women on the basis of their lack of reason.

In defining the threefold goal of the mission—to strengthen faith
through teaching, correct evil, and invite all to baptism—Boniface
demonstrates the relationship between faith and action, belief and
morality. He thus proclaims a Church that is not only "one," "catholic
and apostolic," but also—and perhaps primarily—"holy." In such a
Church, the narratives of the saints including women saints are fit instruments of catechesis and theology. This is not just Boniface's ecclesiology, of course; in proposing Boniface as a saintly example, Rudolf
appropriates this ecclesiology for himself and offers it as the right ecclesiology for Maurus' ninth century diocese of Mainz.

1. The Church is One

One of the important issues to which Rudolf repeatedly alludes is
the way in which Boniface sets up the institutional Church as an instrument of mission. Boniface's goal seems to be to find an appropriate and
effective structure for the promotion of the Gospel and the channeling
of the grace of salvation. He understands a ministerial vocation as a
charism that is given ecclesial status through the acceptance and com-

missioning by ecclesiastical authority. Boniface receives various and successive signs of official approbation: the letter of commission which recognizes his mission to Saxony, ordination to the episcopal See of Fulda, the pallium of metropolitan authority. In turn, Boniface gives official status to Leoba by calling her to a participation in his own mission, thereby confirming the position conferred on her by a prophetic dream. Such official designation insured that the local church of Saxony was the **one Church,** united to the apostles through the representative of Peter in Rome and united in itself under the authority of Boniface. We know from outside sources that the latter worked hard to implement internal structures to foster that unity. He utilized the institution of the synod in his own local church and worked to restore it throughout the Carolingian kingdom.[86] His correspondence shows how often and how carefully he consulted with fellow bishops, asking for advice and support so that their ministry might be truly unified and collegial.[87]

He was mindful that the Church is always in the world and more or less dependent on the goodwill of those in political power. He acquired the support of Charles Martel before assuming his responsibilities in Saxony and, though Rudolf does not tell this part of the story, he does show us the continued interaction between the Carolingian court and the Bonifatian mission. Official support is one thing; continued good will and the ongoing spiritual formation of secular rulers is far more effective for the life of the Church in the long run. Rudolf shows us Leoba's role in that process; she acts as a valued consultant to King Karl (the great) and a spiritual director to his wife. As an unofficial counselor to both king and bishops (as Rudolf says), she continues to promote a good working environment for the missionaries.

2. The Church is Holy
The **holiness** of the Church comes from the presence of Christ within it. Rudolf's presentation of Christ is pervasively relational. He identifies each significant person in his narrative by his or her relationship to Christ and the intimate bonds that bind each believer to Christ is the

---

[86] See Levison, 70–93, and Reuter 69–94.

[87] See *The Letters of Saint Boniface,* trans. Ephraim Emerton (New York: Columbia University Press, 1940).

foundation of their relationships to one another. Because they are committed to Christ in faith, those who believe in him love one another with intimate affection and support one another with gifts, counsel, prayer, and collaborative effort. A bond with Christ is seen particularly in ministerial roles. Because the virgins Leoba and Hadamout are brides of Christ, they are also his consorts, partners with him in the administration of his saving power.[88] The transcendent Christ of faith—Lord, Savior, and Judge—is never beyond the bounds of intimacy, never inaccessible to plea and invocation. He is present to the prayers of believers and, indeed, is present in them. He thus assumes a new humanity, the historical reality of each of his believers, especially those who are themselves "holy." Christ is present in his saints; he is present also in the Word they preach, which Rudolf consistently identifies as a "living word."

Christ is present in both sacrament and miracle, in strikingly similar ways; ordinary human realities—salt, water, rituals of prayer and procession—mediate his saving presence and power. The efficacy of miracles and sacraments brings his saving power to bear on the community assembled to invoke his name; through them, he heals, brings sinners to conversion, restores faith, and unites his followers in that faith. His works validate the truth of his proclamation, as they consistently do in the gospel narratives. They authenticate the probity and virtue of his ministers.

Because Christ lives in his saints, especially Leoba, their humanity continues to demonstrate, as his revealed, the true reality of human nature (destined by God for holiness). Rudolf reveals his vision of this Christified humanity by a careful attention to the delicate balance between nature and grace. Monks and nuns carefully prepare themselves for salvific encounter with the Word of God by cultivating their minds and heart through education and the practice of virtue. The virtues practiced are those dictated by one's state in life; moderation is the mark of all virtues and, in many of Rudolf's stories, excess proves damaging. Natural gifts are nurtured as the presupposition of grace. The institutions that Tetta, Boniface, and Leoba administer as well, as those

---

[88] Elizabeth Johnson does not pursue the metaphors of "partner" and "consort" in *Friends of God and Prophets,* but they are consistent with her understanding of those of "friends" and "companions."

that the latter two set up, give full play to the insights of reason, even as they are constructed to channel the divine word and power.

3. The Church is Catholic

Rudolf places great importance on the character of the mission that Boniface initiates. He shows it to be genuinely collegial, made up of a number of missionaries who represent various important dimensions of Church life. Although all of the missionaries from England shared a cultural background with the Saxons to whom they were sent, Boniface took care to include local persons as well. The ethnic identity of the local population is represented by the person of Sturm, chosen from among them because of his piety and leadership and given special training so that he may be responsible for monastic establishments for men. The mission also represents the full access to salvation that is offered to women in the Church. Leoba, one of the holiest members of the team, is given official status as teacher because of her learning and demonstrates the full salvation and active participation possible for women who respond fully to the call of grace. Rudolf portrays Boniface careful to include both secular and monastic clergy; all possible modes of salvation are visible within the missionaries. The secular clergy represent the promotion of both learning and holiness for the laity who assemble in the churches; monks and nuns represent the call to holiness (and learning) within cloister and monastic chapel. Thus the collegium of missionaries that Boniface assembles reveals the **catholicity** of the Church he preaches, a Church inclusive of ethnically different peoples (like the Jews and Gentiles of old), of women as well as men, and, we may presume, of all social classes (Gal 3:28).[89]

Central to the story of Boniface's collegiality is Rudolf's insistence that Boniface envisioned her as his partner in the mission, emphasized most of all in his giving her his cowl. Boniface's reliance on the support of Anglo-Saxon nuns is well documented in his correspondence and, whatever Rudolf's own ambiguity about the roles of women in his own

---

[89] Rudolf's story says nothing directly about class distinctions, but the correspondence of Boniface shows serious attention to slaves who have accepted the faith and his one extant letter to Leoba concerns a young girl in need of employment for whom Leoba wishes to assure an adequate wage.

church,[90] he does not omit the story nor the subsequent failure of the Fulda monks to fulfill Boniface's last command. Therefore his narrative ultimately shows the full participation, indeed partnership, that Boniface intended. Indeed, as Rudolf describes it, his collegium is really an interconnected web of partnerships, each of them intimate and personal, rather than merely a team of professional relationships. This, I believe, mirrors the Christology of the text; the person of Christ and his intimate relationship with each minister, each baptized member of the Church, is the ground of the institutional relationships that make up the collegium of the local church.

4. The Church is Apostolic

As Rudolf depicts it, Boniface understands the function of the Church in mission as evangelization. This is its primary function, to which all others are subordinate and it is this primacy that identifies the church of Boniface with the church of the apostles. The Church is **apostolic** precisely because it is committed over and above all to proclaiming the living word of God to all people. The missionaries whom Boniface assembles are to teach the word of God and validate that teaching by the holiness of their lives. This emphasis on evangelization within the specific context of the Saxon mission dictates the requirements for ministry. Boniface is well aware that a mere proclamation of the Word will not suffice. Paganism has deep roots within the culture of the indigenous Germanic peoples; previous missions have resulted in few and superficial conversions (as documented by the problems revealed in Boniface's correspondence). What is needed is a deep penetration of the pagan culture by a "distinctive Christian culture"[91] that is fully and completely appropriated. Therefore the missionaries must themselves have absorbed this Christian and literate culture and be competent to teach it. This means not just knowledge of the bible and the literary methods of understanding it—the scientific methods of biblical study of the day. What is also required is a knowledge of the Fathers of the Church, "the decrees of the canons and the laws of the whole ecclesias-

---

[90] See Head, "Integritas," for a brief summary of the debate on whether Rudolf approves the Anglo-Saxon monastic ethos or not.

[91] Greenaway, 33.

tical order," (11) all of which supplied historical context as it was understood in the ninth century. As we have seen, Leoba stands in this text as the epitome of such a teacher, fully prepared academically, devoted to the intellectual apprehension of the faith and with a perceptible holiness that validates her teaching. Her holiness was in turn validated by the miracles that are occasioned by her presence. These miracles function much like the sacraments; they bring the presence of Christ into salvific contact with the community of faith. They also extend a kind of sacramental power into the daily life of the community of faith. Leoba feeds guests and washes their feet, extending the reality of Eucharist into the ordinary intercourse of the people of God. Her miracles extend the realities of sacramental penance, the unction of healing and baptismal conversion, into a community still reluctant in its faith, still bound by the chains of sin.

5. The Inclusion of Leoba

Rudolf thus exposes the four marks of the Church as they are present in their particular way in the local church of Boniface. Central to this presentation is his interpretation of the person of Leoba. Boniface gives her official status and thus her mission is integrated into the unity of the institutional Church; she also furthers the harmonious relationship of the Church with the secular Carolingian power by her work as counsel to both Karl and his wife Hildegarde. By her official presence in the missionary legation, she makes that body more truly catholic, representing both the importance of women in the Church and the opportunities for full salvation and membership to the women she evangelizes. Her ministry as teacher is absolutely central to the primary task of evangelization. She fulfills the plan of Boniface with exactitude: she gives "constant exhortations" to her nuns, to the local people who dwell around her monastery, to bishops, the monks of Fulda and members of the court. She instructs pagans in the faith and teaches "the way of correction" to those under the spell of sin; we see this in the miracle stories where the newly Christian people learn the power and the judgment of Christ. She is Boniface's full partner in the mission and, thus, with him, a representative of the apostles. By her as well as by Boniface, the church of Saxony is given its apostolic character. Finally, she is a medium of Christ to the local church. Christ assumes Leoba's humanity, not, of course, as a new incarnation, but in the same way that he assumes and dwells in the human persons of all those who are baptized into him. Through her, Christ continues to reveal the living Word of God and to offer his saving power; she represents him and, more, becomes his channel of salvation, "a form of salvation" (#11). Her humanity becomes an expression of, indeed an idealization of, a perfect humanity in which nature is fully realized through human effort and perfected by grace, in particular the grace of wisdom. In focusing his story of the missionary Church on her, Rudolf allows Leoba and the women who kept her memory alive a part in his theological conversation. The conversation, indeed, bears the marks of their presence.

4

Baudonivia's Life of Radegunde:
A Theology of Power

Introduction

In the early sixth century in the former Roman province of Gaul, the Christian faith was struggling to get a sure foothold among Germanic tribes that remained largely under the influence of their tribal mores. Certain segments of the Franks who dominated in Gaul had, of course, been associated with the Roman Empire and culture and, de facto, with Christianity for well over a century. The Frank Bauto had become a Roman consul in 385. But others, like Childeric, king of a tribe of eastern Franks and origin of the Merovingian dynasty, only adopted the trappings of the Roman world; he was buried wearing a Roman signet ring and an official Roman robe, over which his non-Roman long hair fell, surrounded with the skeletons of horses sacrificed at his funeral.[1] Officially converted to Christianity in 496, Clovis continued to rule in the style of his fierce ancestors. Gregory of Tours narrates the king's lament in his old age that he had no relatives left to assist him in his last battles; he had eliminated them along the way. As Gregory adds, "He

---

[1] Peter Brown, *The Rise of Western Christendom* (Oxford, U.K.: Blackwell Publications, 1996) 86.

said this, not because he grieved for their deaths, but because in his cunning way he hoped to find some relatives still alive whom he could kill."[2]

Clovis died in 511 and a generation later, when his son Clothar ruled the Franks, little had changed either in the preferred style of kingship or in the limited impact of the Christian Gospel upon the manner of life of aristocratic and royal Franks. It was within this world that St. Radegunde lived, the text of whose life demonstrates genuine theological interest in power, its uses, abuses, and the possibility of its transformation under the sign of the cross.

The historical events of Radegunde's life are a tangle of violence knotted from the many skeins of power to which she was subject and which she sought to control. In 531, when Radegunde was but a child[3] Clothar virtually obliterated her entire family, the rulers of the Thuringians, in an attack against her uncle who broke his treaty with the Franks. She was legitimate booty for the victors and Clothar gambled with his brothers and won her on the battlefield. She was raised on one of his estates until about 541 when he married her, one of the six wives and at least one concubine that Clothar took to his bed. Though she was his wife for about ten years, she bore him no children and left him after he killed her last remaining brother in 550.

She retired to one of the villas, at Saix, that belonged to her by dowry rights and stayed there about eight years until, as Baudoniva narrates, she heard a rumor that the king wished to reclaim her wifely presence. At that moment she fled to Poitiers, negotiating, through Bishop Germanus of Paris, the endowment by Clothar of a convent for women there. The convent at Poitiers was meant to be a refuge but it remained caught up in the continuing narrative of domestic and political violence. The Visigothic princess, Galswinth, passed through on her way to the marriage that ended when she was murdered by her husband and his paramour. Chilperic's daughter, Basina, sought refuge there from

---

[2] *History of the Franks,* bk. 2. ch. 42, trans. L. Thorpe (London: Penguin Books, 1974) 139–40. Cited in Brown, 87.

[3] It is difficult to determine her exact age, but she would not be claimed as a bride for about ten years, so was probably somewhere between six and nine. See Suzanne Wemple, *Women in Frankish Society: Marriage and the Cloister 500–900* (Philadelphia: University of Pennsylvania Press, 1981) 39.

the marriage to Reccared; after Radegunde's death, Basina led an uprising against the new abbess that had to be mediated by a gathering of local bishops. Plunder, rape, and murder marked the entire region around Poitiers throughout Radegunde's life and after her death and her ties of kinship with the many of the principals in the political drama brought her into the heart of the struggles.

The events of these times, places, and people have been narrated and interpreted by numerous authors, contemporary and modern. Radegunde's life was the subject of at least four medieval narratives.[4] Gregory of Tours gives a detailed account of her and her activities in relation to the larger story he is telling of the Christianization of the Franks.[5] Venantius Fortunatus wrote the first separate *vita*;[6] he was an Italian poet who met Radegunde and the Abbess Agnes shortly after his arrival in Poitiers. He remained a close friend of both women for over twenty years and celebrated their affectionate friendship in his occasional poetry. He may have been the author who, with Radegunde's collaboration, wrote the poem "The Thuringian War" about her early trauma and certainly authored the hymn "Vexilla Regis" for the installation of the relic of the Cross in Radegunde's monastery. He ultimately became bishop of Poitiers. He wrote Radegunde's *vita* sometime after her death and several years later Baudonivia, a nun whom Radegunde had nurtured in the monastic life "from the cradle" (as Baudonivia puts it), wrote a second account to include "what the apostolic Bishop Fortunatus . . . omitted in his fear of prolixity."[7]

---

[4] Rene Aigrain, *Sainte Radegunde* (Paris: Librairie Victor Lecoffre, 1918) notes and evaluates the many authors of the lives of this saint.

[5] Gregory tells the story three times. In *The Glory of the Confessors*, trans. Raymond Van Dam (Liverpool: Liverpool University Press, 1988) ch. 104, 105–8; *The Glory of the Martyrs*, trans. Raymond Van Dam (Liverpool: Liverpool University Press, 1988), ch. 5, 22–27; *The History of the Franks*, bk. III, chs. 4–7, 164–69; bk. IX, chs. 39–42, 526–39, bk. VI, ch. 29, 356–58.

[6] Krusch, ed. *MGH,* SRM 2:358–376.

[7] Krusch, ed. *MGH,* SRM 2:377–95. Trans. Jo Ann McNamara and John E. Halborg in *Sainted Women of the Dark Ages* (Durham and London: Duke University Press, 1992) 86–107. Unless otherwise noted, all references to the text are to the McNamara-Halborg trans.

Hildebert of Lavardin took up Radegunde's story again in the twelfth century.[8] For the last two and a half decades, feminist historians, among others, have revisited the texts to ground their interpretations of the social and political world in which Radegunde lived. No matter who tells the story and with what presuppositions, the issue of power remains a key element in the narrative and its interpretations. In the Frankish world, even with its sometimes thin overlay of Christianity, the exercise of power is central to both life and meaning. In this case study, we will investigate the interpretation of power and its exercise that we find in Baudonivia's life of Radegunde against the backdrop of Frankish social and political realities. Of Baudonivia's life, Aigrain writes that "without it we would know nothing or next to nothing about that which gives life to St. Radegunde, her individual countenance, her particular charm, nothing of the resistance to Clothar, nothing of the cult of the relics, the apparitions, the last moments."[9] It is precisely these elements, particular to Baudonivia's life, that constitute something of a theology of power. We will also explore the possibility that Radegunde's devotion to the cross of Christ is the hermeneutic key to her own response to power, as Baudonivia narrates it.

Radegunde in Relation to the *Loci* of Power in the Frankish World

Royal and aristocratic men exercised power in the most obvious ways in the Frankish world. They were warlords who possessed wealth, warriors, and hereditary authority. Theirs was the power of coercion and they used it without qualm. Radegunde's capture and enforced marriage illustrate the violence and force to which even a Christian king had recourse and Gregory of Tours' *History of the Franks* is replete with similar stories. Though he values Frankish rulers for their adherence to Roman, not Arian, Christianity, Gregory deplores their reversion to internecine violence and unequivocally condemns it. His is a moral tale in the Deuteronomic tradition: the Frankish warlords are "men with a mission" and obligated to advance the cause of Christianity. Their ac-

---

[8] *PL* 171, cols. 965A ff.
[9] Aigrain, viii.

tivities as "men of blood" and the retribution they receive demonstrate the prevalence of sin and God's ultimate triumph over it.[10]

Christianity had its own *locus* of power in the Frankish kingdoms, the great Gallo-Roman bishops. Most of the bishops of Gaul were significantly wealthy men. During the turbulent decades of the fifth century, the urban bishops had succeeded to the authority and responsibilities of the old imperial bureaucracy. By the sixth century, they personified law and order, adjudicated local controversies and sought to preserve the peace. They were the high priests of the Christian rituals, enacted in the cathedrals, which unified the local population and gave them their sense of identity. They were also the major benefactors of the city over which they ruled, providing social services, economic and educational opportunities, as well as simple charity. These were all worldly forms of power, from a moral perspective dangerously close to the kind of power exercised by the warlords. But the bishops were mediators of spiritual power as well. The great liturgical actions over which they presided brought the power of God into the Frankish world. In their attempts to locate relics in their own churches and to bring monasteries under their own control Frankish bishops sought to tame the power of God and become its sole mediator.

In the text of Baudonivia, Radegunde represents a third *locus* of power, sharing to some degree the power of the ruling aristocracy and also participating in the administrative functions and mediating power of the bishops. At the same time, Baudonivia shows us Radegunde's commitment of her worldly power, conferred by both birth and marriage, to Christian tasks, in actions that were already traditional and expected of Christian queens.[11] At the end of her very first paragraph, Baudonivia gives us a kind of summary of Radegunde's virtues as a noble laywoman, that is, as a member of the ruling establishment and one who shares their worldly power. "She was a noble sprout sprung

---

[10] J. M. Wallace-Hadrill, *The Barbarian West 400-1000* (London: Basil Blackwell, 1985) 66–68.

[11] See Jo Ann McNamara, "*Imitatio Helenae:* Sainthood as an Attribute of Queenship," *Saints: Studies in Hagiography,* ed. Sandro Sticca (Binghamton, N.Y.: Medieval & Renaissance Texts & Studies, 1996) 51–80.

from royal stock; the nobility she inherited, she adorned the more by her faith."[12]

Baudonivia tells us that Radegunde "inherited nobility," a reflection of the ancient idea that nobility obliges, that aristocratic blood commits a person to play a social and political role that cannot be ignored without serious jeopardy. Baudonivia's statement that Radegunde *adorned* her nobility with faith indicates her understanding that faith cannot excuse one from the political and social obligations of birth and status; faith transforms the natural superiority conferred by aristocratic heredity and enables those who have the *right* to rule the *ability* to rule rightly. Faith does not entirely substitute heavenly goals for earthly goals; rather it subsumes earthly goals (and therefore political and social action) into a transcendent understanding of human life and society. It gives direction to one's political activity, but it does not excuse one from the obligation to act politically. Therefore, the particular virtues that Baudonivia attributes to Radegunde are those appropriate to Radegunde's social status and have political significance; she describes specifically Radegunde's obedience, political vigor and generosity.

"No worldly bonds fettered her but she was girdled about with obedience to God's servants, energetic in redeeming captives and profusely generous with alms to the needy. For she believed that anything that the poor received from her was their own in reality."[13] Radegunde is first praised for her "obedience to God's servants;" by this virtue, Radegunde accepts her true situation in the theoretical structure of Merovingian society. As a Christian queen, she is to further the development and influence of the Church and promote all that pertains to the spiritual well being of the realm. Baudonivia illustrates this kind of obedience with an anecdote. En route to a banquet and adorned with all her worldly display, Radegunde comes upon a place of pagan worship. She orders it burned, displays great personal courage in facing the violent reaction of the pagan Franks and remains there until "the opposing sides had made peace."

[12] "De regali progeniae nobile germen erupit, et quod sumpsit ex genere suo, plus ornavit ex fide." Krusch, 380, ll. 1–2.
[13] "In nullo huius mundi conpede catenata est, in servorum Dei obsequio succincta, in redemptione captivorum sollicita, in egenorum erogatione profusa; proprium credidit, quicquid de se pauper accepit." Ibid., 380, l. 7–9.

It is, perhaps, a distasteful story to modern readers, but Baudonivia's point of view is clear: Radegunde has defended the rights of the Christian faith, even at personal risk to herself, and, not content with destroying an evil, has persevered toward a greater good in making peace. In burning the pagan temple, Radegunde has operated both as a Christian aristocrat and a bishop. Second, Baudonivia affirms that Radegunde is "energetic in redeeming captives." Again, her political position makes her capable of righting the wrongs of society, and her obligation is to use her power to do everything she can to alleviate the suffering of those who suffer the misfortunes of political warfare.

Third, Radegunde is "profusely generous with alms to the needy." This too is a Christian aristocratic obligation in the world; generosity in almsgiving had been a commonplace of spirituality from the beginning.[14] But Baudonivia describes Radegunde as convinced "that anything that the poor received from her was their own in reality;" this reflects a complex understanding of goods and property that was developed by some of the earliest theologians in the classical period.[15] For theologians like Clement of Alexandria (second century A.D.) the earth was created by God for the benefit of all of humanity. Those who were given an abundance of material possessions by the Lord were obliged by that same Lord to see to their equitable distribution. Indeed, for some of the classical early Christian authors, ownership itself, not to say the possession of an excess of goods, constituted a kind of robbery. John Chrysostom regarded the very existence of private property as the consequence of an unjust act in the past. In this view, almsgiving becomes restitution, a concept that St. Ambrose, bishop of Milan, developed in his exegetical letter *De Nabuthe Jezraelita*. For Ambrose, the almsgiver merely returned to the poor man what was originally his because it had been given for the use of all people.

---

[14] Fortunatus is much more detailed about the generosity of Radegunde to the poor. See Jane Tibbetts Schulenburg, *Forgetful of their Sex: Female Sanctity and Society, CA 500-1100* (Chicago and London: The University of Chicago Press, 1998) 68–69.

[15] L. M. Countryman, *The Rich Christian in the Church of the Early Empire: Contradictions and Accommodations* (New York and Toronto: Edwin Mellen Press, 1988) is an introduction to the earliest references.

Baudonivia attributes a variation of this patristic theology to Radegunde the Queen, making her "profuse generosity" an act of political and social justice. We anticipate, therefore, that she will continue to act on behalf of social justice, even within the confines of the ascetical life she chooses. The burning of the pagan temple seems to be a turning point of some kind in Radegunde's life. In Baudonivia's telling of the story, Radegunde immediately initiates a series of steps that will lead her to the monastery of the Holy Cross. But at no point in her life does Radegunde renounce the use of aristocratic power; indeed, she continues to make use of her wealth, her family connections, her knowledge of the power structure and her right to command though her ends remain her own.[16]

Her exercise of worldly power is sometimes used to achieve her own personal freedom. After some time in seclusion at her villa at Saix, Radegunde hears a rumor that the king wants her back as his wife. In order to forestall his plans, she intensifies her personal asceticism and petitions a holy recluse for assistance, sending him a valuable artifact from her royal collection as she requests that he use his prophetic powers to discern her best course of action against the king. In her worldview, such envoys may be sent to the world of the divine, just as spies or messengers are sent to human rulers. The gift may be alms for a holy man or an act of personal renunciation on Radegunde's part. It may also simply be a simple act of customary Frankish diplomacy whereby patronage was exercised through an exchange of valuable gifts.

In relating Radegunde's appeal to the recluse, Baudonivia describes her as pressing the claims of the heavenly King over against that of an earthly king, suggesting something of a royal negotiation. "For she said that if the king truly did want to take her back, she was determined to end her life before she, who had been joined in the embrace of the heav-

---

[16] Wemple, *Women in Frankish Society,* describes the situation in which we may best understand Radegunde's activities in relation to wealth and influential churchmen. "The very nature of a wifely role in an aristocratic family, with its attendant domestic and nurturing activities, gave a woman access to movable wealth—jewels, foodstuffs, articles of clothing, and medicaments—which could be used to cement alliances with bishops and monks" 61. Thus we see Radegunde sending church plate to a recluse and able to engage powerful bishops such at Bishop Germain of Paris.

enly King, would be united again to an earthly king."[17] Having received the holy man's confirmation of her decision, Radegunde then negotiates with Clothar for the building of a monastery at Poitiers, expeditiously accomplished with the help of a bishop and duke who answer to Clothar (5). Much about this incident speaks of Radegunde's skillful use of her worldly power, even in her interactions with the spiritually powerful and her recourse to ascetical discipline.

Somewhat later in her life, she must again face what she perceives to be interference from her royal husband. She seems to have spies of a sort at Clothar's court and receives word from them that Clothar seeks once again to reclaim her (6). Once more she begins to employ all the human resources at her disposal. She writes official letters ("sacramentales") and employs her agent Proculus to take them "secretly" to the Bishop Germanus of Paris. Powerfully moved, whether by her holiness or the information in the letters, Bishop Germanus quickly brings Clothar to repentance and he formally asks the queen's pardon, using the Bishop as intermediary. From this point on, he will allow Radegunde the freedom to follow her religious intentions, in the accomplishment of which she will continue to use her worldly resources. When war breaks out among the kings, she will engage in the usual strategies of diplomacy as well as in prayer and penance to bring about the necessary peace.

When she seeks to acquire the relic of the true cross and have it installed in her monastery at Poitiers, she engages the support of various kings, the emperor in Constantinople and several bishops to achieve her end. Though I will argue that the text of Baudonivia is about the inversion of power and/or its transformation, we must first note the ways in which Radegunde exercises worldly power, composed of wealth, status and personal connections with other powerful people, before we can understand its inversion.

Into this context we must, perhaps, put a small and rather confusing miracle told by Baudonivia. The story of Vinoberga comes just before Baudonivia narrates the efforts that Radegunde makes to acquire relics, culminating in the acquisition of the relic of the cross. Baudonivia introduces it with the affirmation that the miracle is "in praise of Christ, who

---

[17] "Quod si hoc rex vellet, ipsa ante optaret vitam finire, quam regi terreno iterum iungi, quia iam Regis caelestis copulabantur amplexus." Krusch, 381, ll. 13–14.

makes His own [servants] cause fear in other [people]."[18] Vinoberga is a
convent housemaid who "with bold daring presumed to sit in the chair of
the blessed queen after her death."[19] She is described as "rash" as well as
presumptuous and is punished by a fire that burns, without consuming,
"for three days and three nights." Finally Vinoberga yells out a prayer of
repentance and petition, in which "the whole population" joins her and
Radegunde quenches the fire. Is Vinoberga rash and presumptuous because, as a housemaid she takes the chair of the foundress, an aristocrat?

Is this a story about status?[20] Certainly the chair was the traditional
symbol of one's authority. Perhaps the author wishes to teach that,
while the mighty may forgo earthly status through humility, such status
may not be ignored by the lower classes with impunity. Or does the
housemaid's action indicate her lack of faith in Radegunde's sanctity? If
so, she thereby impugns, not Radegunde, but the power of God and is
punished, appropriately, by the fire which symbolizes both God's transcendent presence and the purification required of all those who seek it.
In either case, Radegunde saves Vinoberga from her penalty. If Vinoberga's fault was a lack of faith in Radegunde, her prayer to that saint for
relief signifies her "conversion." If her sin is arrogance, then she is well
purified by the fires; as Baudonivia says, "Such a punishment [not the
miracle itself!] made everyone cautious and more devout."

Radegunde's Holiness as a Source of Power

If indeed Baudonivia shows a Radegunde who continues to use aristocratic power, she leaves no doubt that the real basis of her power is her
holiness. In the text noted in the introduction to this book, Carolyn Heilbrun notes how critical the issue of power is in women's biographies and
autobiographies. She points out that while the acquisition and use of
power is central to the biographies of men, authors of the lives of women
and, often the women who are themselves the subjects of such narrated

[18] "Adiciatur et aliud ad laudem Christi miraculum, qui suos trepidare aliis facit."
Ibid., 385, ll. 30–31.
[19] "Vinoberga una ex eius fuit famulabus, qui ausu temerario in cathedra beatae
reginae post eius discessum sedere praesumpsit." Ibid., ll. 31–32.
[20] Such is Wemple's interpretation, 165.

lives, are often deeply troubled about a woman's relationship to power. But in medieval saints' lives the issue is more complex than can be explained by gender alone. The hagiographical tradition repeatedly documents the tension between spiritual power (considered real power in the world of the saints) and human (political) power that, ideally, implements the divine will, but is, in reality, more often in conflict with that will. Access to *real power*—divine power—is achieved through the abnegation of political power and by humility. Through all the conflicts that Radegunde must negotiate in order to create and maintain her monastery, she experiences the tensions and dilemmas within the dynamics of divine and human power for one who would be both saint and queen.

Baudonivia demonstrates several ways in which Radegunde attempts to resolve the tension between human and divine power. One of these is Radegunde's consistent recourse to asceticism precisely at moments when she has marshaled the resources of her worldly identity. In the opening paragraphs of Baudonivia's text in which she describes Radegunde's married life, she shows us Radegunde practicing the virtues consistent with her state in life as married aristocrat. Although Baudonivia says that in her spirit she showed the monastic virtues she would later commit to, she names the virtues of a good aristocratic laywoman: obedience, the energetic redemption of captives and generous almsgiving. We first see her recourse to a stricter asceticism when she has retired from Clothar to her villa at Saix. As she is about to confront the king with her refusal to return to him, she adopts a regime of stricter fasts, vigils, prayer, and hair shirts. "Hearing this, the blessed one shook with terror and surrendered herself to the harsher torment of the roughest of hair shirts which she fitted to her tender body. In addition, she imposed torments of fasting upon herself, and spent her nights in vigils pouring out prayers. For she scorned to rule her fatherland and she rejected the sweetness of marriage; excluding worldly love, she chose exile lest she wander from Christ."[21]

---

[21] "Haec audiens beatissima, nimio terrore perterrita, se amplius cruciandam tradidit cilicio asperrimo ac tenero corpori aptavit; insuper et ieiunii cruciationem indixit, vigiliis pernoctans, in oratione se tota diffudit, despexit sedem patriae, vicit dulcedinem coniugis, exclusit caritatem mundialem, elegit exsul fieri, ne peregrinaretur a Christo." Krusch, 381, ll. 1–5. Surely there is some irony in Baudonivia's statement that Radegunde has rejected the "sweetness" of marriage.

She is acting here out of "terror;" determined to remain free of her husband, she may well be attempting to make herself less attractive to him through her ascetical practice. She may also be afraid that she will let herself be persuaded to return; it could be her own desires that she seeks to deaden with penance. The reference to exile and wandering suggests that she is influenced by the notion of penance and pilgrimage promulgated by the Celtic monks who were great spiritual influences in Francia from the fifth century on.

Then, when Radegunde has succeeded in establishing the monastery at Poitiers, she makes an explicit renunciation of power. She refuses to be the monastic abbess, "reserving no authority of her own in order to follow the footsteps of Christ more swiftly . . . ."[22] In describing the foundation of the monastery, Baudonivia employs two metaphors that speak to the way in which Radegunde transforms the wealth that was hers by family and rank; by extension, these metaphors indicate also the transformation of the power that wealth provided. She describes the queen as gathering the women of the monastery, so many jewels ("ornaments") in her new treasury. Every royal woman had a cache of jewels that constituted her own wealth and enabled her to enact her will with luxurious gifts. In the preceding paragraph, Baudonivia tells how she sent one such jeweled object to the holy recluse she consulted. In building the monastery, Radegunde has replaced the traditional jewel hoard with the devout women she has gathered in the community. "There she would seek to gather ornaments of perfection, a great congregation of maidens for the deathless bridegroom Christ."[23] Baudonivia also describes Radegunde's transferal of authority to the Abbess Agnes in terms of assets and debits; in giving the abbacy to Agnes, Radegunde subtracts assets from her earthly account and adds them to her heavenly account.[24] The image is that of a good administrator keeping accurate household accounts. And like a provident steward, Radegunde sees her assets increase: the jewels

[22] "Quo electa abbatissa, etiam constituta, tam se quam sua omnia ei tradidit subdita potestate, et ex proprio iure nihil sibi reservans, ut curreret expedita post Christi vestigia. . . ." Ibid ll. 24–26.

[23] ". . . ubi perfectionis ornamenta conquireret et magnam congregationem puellarum Christo numquam moritaro sponso." Ibid., ll. 22–24.

[24] "plus augeret in caelo, quanto magis subtraxisset de saeculo." Ibid., ll. 26–27.

that are the community "began to glow" in humility, charity, chastity, and fasting. "Certainly soon her holy ways began to glow in the act of humility, in the fruitfulness of charity, in the splendor of chastity, and in the richness of fasting. With all her love, she gave herself up to her celestial spouse. . . ."[25]

In describing these virtues Baudonivia uses both the language of fertility and of wealth—"fruitfulness," "splendor," and "richness"—as she speaks of Christ as the bridegroom.[26] Here Radegunde's abnegation, the renunciation of her authority to another, has transformed both her ruling power and her marital status into religious relationships that produce a different kind of prosperity and a different order of kinship. The monastery becomes the base of a different and higher level of power—holiness—and its members become the progeny she did not produce with her human husband Clothar. Not that she will be able to eschew worldly power from this point on. But, again, each time she must do so, Baudonivia describes how she intensifies her personal self-abnegation.

When she successfully engages Bishop of Germanus of Paris in her efforts to free herself from further interference by Clothar, Baudonivia says that the office of vigils was added to the daily schedule and "[Radegunde] made herself the guard of her body, as if of a prison, for the night vigils. And although she was merciful to others, she became the judge of herself; she was pious to the rest, but severe to herself in abstinence; generous to all, but restrained for herself, so that exhaustion by

[25] "Mox etiam eius sancta conversatio coepit fervere in humilitatis conversatione, in caritatis ubertate, in castitatis lumine, in iieiuniorum pinguedine, et ita se toto amore caelesti tradidit Sponso. . . ." Ibid., ll. 27–382, l. 2.

[26] Baudonivia uses the verb "tradidit" to describe Radegunde's gift of herself to Christ. It is the word used in the institution narrative and the Eucharistic Prayer to indicate Christ's gift of himself to the Father on the cross. This connection of Radegunde to the gospel narratives of the Passion is important to the theme of service, developed below.

fasting was not sufficient, unless she triumphed over her body."[27] When she enters into negotiations between those different kings at war with one another, she requests her sisters to engage in "constant vigils" and prayers for peace. And, finally, her strategy remains the same when she struggles to bring a relic of the true cross to Poitiers.[28]

One must acknowledge that such references to severe asceticism can be problematic on two counts. One, they are admittedly the conventional descriptions given to all the saints in medieval hagiography. Second, asceticism has been interpreted by many as the way in which women, influenced by the dualism and misogyny of Christianity, denigrated their own body and worth. Both criticisms have some validity and, for the first, there is no doubt that Baudonivia is influenced to some degree by the conventions of the genre. The question, then, is whether or not she intends anything specific to Radegunde's life—beyond affirming her conventional holiness—by recourse to those conventions. As for the attempt by early Christian women to express self-hatred through extreme asceticism, such criticism is given weight by modern studies that link self-destructive behavior to the early experience of violence, such as that experienced by Radegunde. But one must, *a fortiori*, be extremely cautious about applying research done on modern women to a much earlier historic period, since the prevailing mores greatly shape how people experience their life events. We must note, here, that the earlier *vita* of Radegunde, that penned by Venantius Fortunatus, gives significant and detailed emphasis to Radegunde's asceticism while in Baudonivia's life her austerities are somewhat minimized and given a different context. In

---

[27] "Talibus ergo rebus intenta, addito vigiliarum ordine, quasi carceris se sui corporis fecit pernoctando custodem. Et cum esset aliis misericors, sibi iudex effecta est, reliquis pia, in se abstinendo severa, omnibus larga, sibi restricta, ut madefecta ieiuniis non sufficeret, nisi et de suo corpore triumpharet." Krusch 382, l. 28–31.

[28] "She cast herself into agonies of fasts and vigils lamenting and wailing with her whole flock every day until at last the Lord respected his handmaid's humility and moved the heart of the king to do judgment and justice in the midst of the people." "In quanto se cruciatu posuit, in geiuniis, in vigiliis, in profusione lacrimarum, tota congregatio sua in luctu et fletu omnibus diebus, usquequo respexit Dominus humilitatem ancillae suae, qui dedit in corde regis ut faceret iudicium et iustitiam in medio populi?" Ibid., 389, ll. 4–7.

fact, one must ask why Baudonivia includes them at all, since she says she is not going to repeat what Fortunatus has written. We must assume that her inclusion of the ascetical theme serves a specific purpose in her text and therefore cannot be omitted, even at the risk of repetition. Therefore, the context in which she refers to them is important and, with one exception, those references are always linked to Radegunde's exercise of secular and aristocratic power.

One may conclude, at least as a working hypothesis, that Baudonivia intends to demonstrate that, although Radegunde the queen may exploit her own worldly resources, she does so with great care, using asceticism to insure that she is putting those resources at the service of God's will. If so, then Baudonivia's assessment of ascetical practice is not intrinsically linked to a hatred of the body, whatever Radegunde's own attitudes may have been. For Baudonivia, Radegunde's asceticism demonstrates, not just generic holiness, but the specific holiness of a queen who transforms worldly power into the power of God.

Baudonivia demonstrates the power of Radegunde's holiness in many ways, including the presence of miracles while she is alive as well as after her death. This is not the place to discuss the extensive play given to miracle stories in the lives of saints and many other medieval texts; that theme has been well treated by Benedicta Ward in *Miracles and the Medieval Mind*.[29] Augustine encouraged the publicizing of miracles, particularly those associated with saints, because he believed that they stimulated the faith of those who believed and confounded those who didn't. Ward affirms that miracles were central to the worldview of the Middle Ages; it was universally accepted that the miraculous was "a basic dimension of life. The bounds of reality included the unseen in a way alien to modern thought."[30] This does not mean that miracles were simply retold reverently and without secondary purposes on the part of the author. Indeed, Ward discusses monastic miracles as "propaganda," publicized to promote the importance of shrines and inspire pilgrimage. Often the narrator intends to demonstrate through the miracle that

[29] Benedicata Ward, *Miracles and the Medieval Mind* (Philadelphia: University of Pennsylvania Press, 1987).

[30] Ward, 33.

the biblical story of salvation was continued in the "later days" and new cultural context of other saints.

Seen against this complex horizon, the purpose of Baudonivia' miracle stories becomes a bit more clear. For the most part, they are designed simply to show Radegunde's sanctity, to demonstrate that she has been seized by the saving power of God to such fullness that she can now mediate that power to others. They are also part of the attempt of those who admire her to promote her own places as sacred shrines. The matron Mammezo is healed at the oratory Radegunde established even though the saint is still living and is not present at the shrine. Posthumous miracles attest to the healing power to be found at the basilica that is her burial place. Baudonivia makes clear these intentions when she exclaims, "how bountiful and rich is the mercy of God that makes His own fold stand in awe of Him and seeks out the places where He may show His power to the faithful as the giver and dispenser of virtues." Her words echo Augustine's thought. But most of all, the miracles demonstrate the inversion of power that takes place in the spiritual world of the saints. It is when Radegunde renounces the status of queen that the miracles begin. By abandoning her access to coercive power, Radegunde creates the possibility for divine power to be active.

The Power of Holiness for Women and By Women: the Monastery

Nowhere is Radegunde's transformation of power more evident than in her foundation of the monastery at Poitiers and the leadership she exercises there. First, the monastery itself, as we have seen, is a place founded through an astute use of worldly power joined to religious purposes. It was a place where power was specifically exercised on behalf of women who were otherwise without significant power in the Frankish kingdom. The convent was a refuge, a place protected by the holiness of St. Radegunde and a power base from which Radegunde and other women could engage in the struggles of the day.

1. The Convent as Refuge

A key moment in Baudonivia's narration tells of Radegunde's move from her own private refuge at Saix to the foundation of a monastery at Poitiers. The move was, of course, for her own protection. An officially established monastery was somewhat less vulnerable to manipulation by the king than a villa, even if owned in her own name. Nonetheless, the foundation at Poitiers also provided the same protection for other women that Radegunde was seeking for herself and in that way was an act of empowerment in a world that offered precious little power to women. Jo Ann McNamara has pointed out that one of the many socially important roles that convents played in the early Middle Ages, was that of shelter and refuge for women who were abused and in danger.[31] Radegunde's monastery, for instance, became a refuge for Chilperic's daughter Basina, when her mother fell out of favor with the king.[32] Convents also allowed women to escape the physical dangers of childbirth and the sorrows of frequent infant mortality as well as the spiritual dangers and sorrows connected with the temptations of sexual intercourse.

Radegunde's first biographer Fortunatus was eloquent on these dangers and the rewards waiting for those who escaped them in the monastic life.[33] Several of the miracles that Baudonivia narrates speak to monastery as refuge and to the protective power of Radegunde over the monastery and its women. Baudonivia tells how, after the sisters have gone to sleep, Radegunde spends the night in prayer. It is a protective vigil that Baudonivia describes: "With her holy right hand, she would protect her monastery with the sign of the cross" (18). At the sign of the cross, multitudes of demons "in the form of goats" vanished. On another occasion, "a raucous night bird" is expelled, again with the sign of the cross and the invocation of "Lady Radegunde" (19). These are symbolic stories that demonstrate Radegunde's provision of a safe refuge for women in the monastery at Poitiers. In providing that safe haven, Radegunde was ready to use all the worldly power she possessed as well as the spiritual power she could acquire by sanctity.

2. The Convent as Opportunity

Besides being a refuge, a monastery was an institution that allowed women to develop their own power and resources. It provided them

---

[31] Jo Ann McNamara, "Living Sermons: Consecrated Women and the Conversion of Gaul," in *Peaceweavers,* ed. Lillian Thomas Shank and John Al Nichols (Kalamazoo, Mich.: Cistercian Publications, 1987) 19–37.

[32] Gregory of Tours tells her story in *The History of the Franks,* bk. 5, ch. 39, 303–5.

[33] See Wemple, 150–51.

with educational and administrative possibilities lacking even to women of wealth and status. It gave the women who entered there an empowering experience of female solidarity and it allowed them to learn from their own experience rather than merely to follow the rules set by men for their behavior. Radegunde was not content to create only a safe physical space for the women of Holy Cross, but established an ordered environment where learning and wisdom could be honed through specifically feminine experience, where the established tradition could be recast through "oral exchanges" in a community of women voluntarily assembled.

Education was a source of power, both within the Frankish aristocratic world and, especially, within the spiritual world of Christian faith. By acquiring literacy, Frankish rulers and magnates were able more and more to enter into the world of law and government that was the legacy of the Roman empire they aspired to achieve and we see how Radegunde uses the power of the written word to achieve her ends. She writes official letters ("sacramentales") to secure her own autonomy, to establish the monastery, to promote peace among the various kings and, finally, to secure relics for Poitiers, especially the relic of the cross. Baudonivia shows the saintly queen even more concerned about the acquisition of literacy in the service of the faith. The Christian ethos affirmed the importance of biblical literacy for a religious faith rooted in a sacred text; yet that literacy, and consequently the full experience of faith, was generally accessible to women only in the monastic situation. The choice of a cloistered life was, among other things, a choice to live at the heart of the world of the spirit and the possibility inherent within a biblical education was one of the things that made the choice of the cloister attractive. Though not an abbess—Baudonivia has noted that she refused to assume that role in the monastery—Radegunde assumes a leadership role in the formation and education of the nuns and by her example demonstrates both the importance and the empowering possibilities within a Christian education.

Baudonivia particularly emphasizes Radegunde's dedication to the study of Scripture. She notes that Radegunde ordered reading during meals, insisted on reading and "incessant daily preaching" along with prayers and almsgiving to combat "slovenliness" and to obviate ignorance as an excuse for mediocrity. No mention is made of who is to do the preaching, but the biographer records, in several places, that Rade-gunde herself preached, even while she was asleep! Presumably then, it was the nuns themselves, at least those with authority and wisdom, who were to preach to and teach the others. She repeats in several places that Radegunde read the scriptures incessantly and, when she was forced to take a little rest, had the psalms continuously read to her. Though devo-tion to scripture was a hagiographical commonplace, Baudonivia testi-fies to its reality in Radegunde's life by relating a little story in which the queen, wishing to hail the portress, calls out "alleluia" instead of the nun's name (8). Her mind is so thoroughly filled with biblical texts that they slip out inappropriately in ordinary conversation.

Radegunde seeks not only to teach her sisters that they must read; she attempts to teach them also how to understand and interpret what they read. "When the lesson had been read, she would say, with careful attention to our souls: 'If you do not understand what is read, why don't you search for it diligently in the mirror of your souls?'"[34] Baudonivia here passes on the hermeneutic principle that Radegunde had taught. She bade her sisters search for the meaning of the scriptures "in the mir-ror of [their] souls." This means, first, that the meaning of Scripture is to be found in the religious experience they produce. It is not academic meaning that is sought, but the lived meaning. It also indicates that Radegunde referred the sisters to the wisdom of the Spirit who dwells within the soul, the One who interprets the Word of God because She is the Spirit of that Word. Finally, it suggests a reference to the soul as con-taining the image of God, in Augustine's teaching; since all of Scripture reveals God, it is the presence of God in the soul that can interpret the divine meaning. With all of these nuances, however, ultimately it is ex-perience that is the hermeneutical key to her interpretation of the bibli-cal texts. The texts were authoritative only in so far as they illuminated, and were illuminated by, the experience of life. Her monastic spiritual-ity was not a slavish following of rules but a careful and discerning in-terpretation of her own life in the light of the wisdom of the tradition and of the shared understanding of the community.

---

[34] "Si non intellegitis quod legitur, quid est, quod non sollicite requiritis specu-lum animarum vestrarum?" Krusch, 384, ll. 1–2.

A brief comment from Baudonivia illustrates Radegunde's commitment to the hermeneutic of experience. When visiting clerics come to the monastery, she questions them on their own spiritual practices and understanding of Christian life ("manner of serving the Lord"). She then tries out their suggestions herself before passing on the teaching to the community. Before she passed on such wisdom to others, however, she tested it in the crucible of her own experience. Only then, would she distill her experience into words that became more meaningful for having first been exemplified in the life of the queen. Tested by experience and dramatized in her example, her verbal recommendations gain force.

In addition to the possibilities for an education that privileged their own experience and inner guidance by the Spirit, the women of Radegunde's monastery were empowered by an experience of female solidarity. Most of the extant documentation narrates the experience of aristocratic and royal women, but there are indications that women of lesser rank were included in the benefits available in Radegunde's convent. The quaint story of Vinoberga indicates the presence of servants in the community and the story of her burial contains a reference to "female serfs" who carry candles before her body in the funeral procession. One may logically assume that the serfs were in service to the monastery although they are not members of the congregation since they are free to leave the enclosure as the nuns are not. Beyond this, it is difficult to determine the specific distinctions of aristocrats and servants within the Poitiers monastery because of Baudonivia's theme that Radegunde herself became a servant within the monastery (about which more later).

It may well be that Baudonivia herself is one of those of lesser rank. In the conventional self-disclaimer that the author makes at the beginning of the text she disparages her writing as "non politus sed rusticus." She writes, as she says, with a peasant's hand (later critics concur with her judgment[35]); perhaps this refers to her rank as well as to her style. The author does however make the assertion that Radegunde has exchanged the community of sisters for her blood relations and considers them genuinely her family. In a Germanic context this is a powerful affirmation; family was the firmest human bond in the Germanic social

---

[35] Wemple notes that in introducing his edition of her text Krusch calls her style "barbarous," *Women in Frankish Society,* 183.

order and would remain so for many more centuries. It was the source of identity, of wealth and, especially, of security. But according to Baudonivia, Radegunde found all of these now in her community. Rank and social distinctions may remain in the community—as they do in a family—but they do not abrogate the kinship bonds that now bind Radegunde to her sisters.

After Radegunde's death, Baudonivia sought to assess the legacy that she began to see more clearly in hindsight. A touch of humanity graces her narrative here; she notes that the sisters did not always respond fervently to the founder's admonitions during her lifetime. It is only in retrospect (and, especially, in the turmoil after her death) that they appreciated fully the wisdom of her leadership. Not surprisingly, Baudonivia emphasizes the way in which Radegunde shaped the religious and community life of the convent at Poitiers. Though Radegunde had probably adopted the Rule of Caesarius of Arles in founding her monastery, it was a very flexible instrument, as religious rules remained for several centuries. Under that rule, the insight and wisdom of the founder and early abbesses gave to each foundation its individual character. Baudonivia lauds Radegunde particularly for the way in which she promoted the spiritual and intellectual formation of the community. Certainly, Baudonivia sees Radegunde as the convent's protective force, a kind of spiritual shield that stands between the convent and all outside threat. The stories of her nightly vigils and blessings are but exemplifications of the kind of spiritual protection that Baudonivia attributes to the guiding presence of Radegunde.

Radegunde's concern for the safety and well being of women and her exercise of power on their behalf last beyond her life. The miracle stories demonstrate a special concern for afflicted women. Beside the story of Vinoberga, there is the cure of Mammezo. The last complete story that Baudonivia tells is also an example of engendered power, of Radegunde acting again on behalf of women neglected in a man's world and a man's church. It occurs on the feast of St. Hilary when the custom of the city of Poitiers is for all the monasteries to gather at St. Hilary's Basilica to celebrate the vigils together, after which each community returns to their own church to complete the office of the saint. Two women gravely troubled by evil spirits (one has suffered for fifteen years) rave, roar and clamor all night in Hilary's church. Indeed, they stand out among a large group of demoniacs assembled there because they are "gravely infested" and rave violently to the point of shaking the building. The narrative details reflect the tendency to view women as vulnerable to demonic influence and dangerous instruments of demonic power. Baudonivia specifically notes that the women are not healed at the shrine of St. Hilary; they follow the monks and abbot to Radegunde's basilica, the church "that Radegunde had loved so well" (27), where her power is invoked and they are cured. As Baudonivia editorializes, "Some [of the many afflicted] were liberated at the holy man's basilica while others [especially two very troubled women] were brought to Lady Radegunde's basilica for, as they were equal in grace, so were they both shown equal in virtue."[36] Hilary and Radegunde are equal in sanctity and equally protectors of the city, but Radegunde's holy protection falls in a particular way on afflicted women, a point that Baudonivia does not affirm but suggests by the way she tells the story.

Finally, Baudonivia notes that "female serfs," each of whom carries a candle bearing her own name attend Radegunde's funeral procession. When a debate ensues over the placement of those candles, one of them flies out of the hand of the *boy* (to whom they have been handed over at the gravesite) and flies to the feet of the dead saint. This decides the issue and the name of the woman, Calva, whose candle it was is recorded for all posterity. As a miracle story, it is slight. As a story about status and gender, both of which Baudonivia carefully details, it is intriguing. Though men are in charge of the burial rites (bishops preside and male servants take control of the candles once they arrive at the chosen site of St. Mary's Basilica), it is female serfs who have the privilege of processing in front of the bier. Do they represent the nuns who are prevented from this honor by the rule of enclosure? Do they represent Radegunde herself who, in humility, renounced her royal status to become "a pauper for the Lord?" Peter Brown in *The Cult of the Saints*[37] has examined

---

[36] "Ad basilicam sancti viri sunt alii liberati, alii vero basilicae dominae Radegundis sunt directi, ut, sicut aequalis gratiae erant, ita aequalis et virtus ostenderetur," Krusch, 394, ll. 31–32.

[37] Peter Brown, *The Cult of the Saints* (Chicago: The University of Chicago Press, 1981). See also Patrick J. Geary, *Furta Sacra: Thefts of Relics in the Central Middle Ages* (Princeton, The University Press, 1978).

how processions to the graves of the martyrs in the Late Antique empire allowed the Christian community to restructure itself in the marginal ground of the cemetery. There, women, the poor, the crippled, and dispossessed jostled the arms of the wealthy and aristocratic, "on terms equal in everything but status."[38] All had equal access to the power of the holy ones, an experience of human solidarity that was unavailable anywhere else. Baudonivia's narrative suggests a similar experience that is rooted in the life and holiness of Radegunde.

Holiness as Power Beyond the Monastery

Radegunde's holiness empowered her for activities beyond the monastery. She created "safety and closure" to be sure, but her safe and enclosed space continued to be the venue of "action," "experience," and "life," for her and for many of those who joined her. The dramas enacted at Poitiers were part and parcel of the political and social action of the Merovingian world. The miracle just above suggests that her influence was important in the city of Poitiers and Baudonivia tells of her involvement in the political wars of the region. Wars were endemic in Radegunde's world and as a member of one royal family by birth and another through marriage she was inevitably drawn into various conflicts. But according to Baudonivia, Radegunde engages herself beyond mere familial obligations. Most significantly, she refuses to take sides in the conflict. Her prayers were for the lives of *all* the kings who were engaged in warfare all around her and she prayed "for their stability." She well knew that the devastations of war fell most heavily on the land itself and the general population and therefore political "stability" rather than the success of one warring faction over another was the most important outcome.

Though she prayed and did penance to this end, she also engaged in the exercise of her political and spiritual power in pursuing it. Baudonivia tells us that she wrote to all the kings as soon as she heard of bitterness beginning to arise among them; obviously she kept her ear to the ground, as it were, and may herself have engaged spies so that she could forestall conflicts at their inception. "And, likewise, she sent to their noble followers to give the high kings salutary counsel so that their

---

[38] Brown, 45.

power might work to the welfare of the people and the land." By "noble followers," Baudonivia refers here to the magnates who acted as royal counselors, an institution of political and moral importance much commented on under the Carolingians but already significant in Merovingian times.

Radegunde is attempting to bring her moral vision to bear on the political struggles of the various kings, not only directly, but also through the established lines of political advisement. Clearly she engages in skillful diplomacy and Baudonivia attributes great success to her efforts although history records that the peace she helped establish was quite transitory. According to Jacques Fontaine, in narrating the story of Radegunde's peacemaking, Baudonivia introduces a new theme into traditional hagiography, that of the saintly queen's contribution to her country.[39] It is of a piece with Baudonivia's theme that holiness can empower a woman efficaciously, enabling her to influence all those earthly forces upon which the common good of human communities depend.

To this same end, Radegunde takes on the work of bringing relics to Poitiers. Recent scholarship has greatly illuminated the meaning and importance of relics, of their transfer from one place to another and of the installation ceremonies that solemnized their arrival. Benedicta Ward connects the tradition of miracle narratives to the development of relic-bearing shrines. Peter Brown, quoted above, situates the early devotion to relics within the late antique Roman culture of client and patron relationships. Having explored the way in which the posthumous *presence* of the saint was held to be accessible to the devout through shrines and relics, Brown explains that "if relics could travel, then the distance between the believer and the place where the holy could be found ceased to be a fixed, physical distance. It took on the shifting quality of late-Roman social relationships: distances between groups and persons were overcome by gestures of grace and favor, and the dangerously long miles of imperial communications system were overcome by a strenuously maintained ideology of unanimity and concord."[40]

[39] As cited in Jane Tibbetts Schulenburg, "Saints' Lives as a Source for the History of Women," *Medieval Women and the Sources of Medieval History,* ed. Joel T. Rosenthal (Athens and London: The University of Georgia Press, 1990) 299 and n. 57.

[40] Brown, *The Cult of the Saints,* 89.

The arrival of relics from Rome often signified the connection between the new and distant Germanic church to its center and source, a kind of spiritual aqueduct between the Roman headwaters and the new fields of the Lord, waiting to be watered then harvested. The venerable Bede records the pattern as it affected the Anglo-Saxon churches in his *Ecclesiastical History*. The translation of relics both conferred status on the new church and required it to transcend its tribal understanding of itself. Once a local shrine possessed relics of a saint from "outside," it had to begin to think of itself as "Roman," that is, as part of a larger universe of communities. Brown particularly underscores the way in which the cult of relics in Merovingian Gaul was celebrated with what he calls a "studiously all-inclusive ceremonial." Using texts from Gregory of Tours, Venantius Fortunatus and Victricius—authors who are also among our sources for the life of Radegunde—Brown describes how "the festival of a saint was conceived of as a moment of ideal consensus on a deeper level. It made plain God's acceptance of the community as a whole: his mercy embraced all its disparate members, and could reintegrate all who had stood outside in the previous year."[41]

It is within the context explored by Brown that Radegunde's aggressive pursuit of relics makes the most sense. Baudonivia records that it was while she was still at Saix that "she *determined . . .* to collect relics of all the saints [emphasis mine]" and when she entered her monastery she continued to gather "a great multitude of the saints" from all four corners of the earth. The acquisition of relics is, for Radegunde, a lifelong commitment that culminates in her efforts to acquire a relic of the true cross. This relic would most firmly link the church at Poitiers with both Jerusalem and Rome and, thereby, with the whole world; it would also bring the personal presence of the redeeming Lord and universal savior to Poitiers in a particularly powerful way. To acquire it, therefore, Radegunde brooks no obstacle. To acquire other relics, she had prayed, fasted and begged. To posses a relic of the true cross, she took counsel with King Sigebert, importuned the emperor, and when thwarted by the citizens of Poitiers who do not seem to want the relic, she fasts, wails, keeps vigil and again appeals to the king who sends a royal warrior to

---

[41] Ibid., 99–100.

achieve Radegunde's desire. In describing Radegunde's efforts on behalf of relics, Baudonivia emphasizes that she acts as both queen and as pastor. She repeatedly parallels Radegunde's pursuit of the relic of the cross with those of St. Helena. When thwarted, she does not exemplify any of the meekness with which she seems to have served everyone in her monastery; Baudonivia says "her spirit blaz[ed] in a fighting mood" and she exhibits all of the fierceness of a royal Thuringian in getting her way.

For her, the presence of the cross in Poitiers will ensure not only great religious blessings but "the welfare of the whole fatherland and the stability of [Sigebert's] kingdom," as she said in her petition to the king. Brown has shown how the cult of holy relics served both political peace and social inclusiveness. Radegunde's spiritual power and that of the relics represented a particular form of justice, well understood in the Merovingian world. As Brown says, Christians in Gaul "turned the celebration of the memory of the martyrs into a reassuring scenario by which unambiguously good power, associated with the amnesty of God and the *praesentia* of the martyr, overcame the ever-lurking presence of evil power."[42] Therefore, bringing the cross to Poitiers is simply another way in which Radegunde works assiduously for the peace of the people over whom she has never ceased to be queen.[43] When the relic finally is enshrined in her own monastery, Baudonivia calls her "this best provider, this good shepherdess." In facilitating the dispensation of divine power, Radegunde has exercised her own power, at once royal and pastoral, the power of the holy.

[42] Ibid., 101.

[43] Neither the importance of Radegund's miracles nor belief in her special protective power in the region of Poitiers ceased with the end of the Middle Ages. Jean Filleau in *La Preuve Historique des Litanies de la grande Reyne de France, Sainte Radegonde* (Poitiers: Abraham Mounin Imprimeur et Libraire, 1943) 207–13, details the continual protection of the saint. In 1450, she helps Poitiers defend itself against the English and a procession is instituted to honor this protection. In 1569, her tomb inspires the soldiers of Poitiers to withstand the assault of 50,000 Calvinists. In 1643, it was proposed that Radegund be made patroness not only of Poitiers but of the whole kingdom and be honored by appropriate observances on her feast day. According to René Aigrain, the women of Poitiers sought her protection against an invasion of the Prussians in 1871 and her tomb was an important pilgrimage site in World War I.

The ambivalence toward power in Baudonivia's text has already been noted. She praises Radegunde for eschewing the worldly power of queen, yet portrays her as completely the queen in her aggressive pastoring of her flock at Poitiers. She describes how, in humility, Radegunde foregoes the role of abbess, yet praises her for giving the sisters rules and admonitions, leadership and teaching. Perhaps Brown's analysis of relic rituals and Radegunde's fierce pursuit of relics help us understand this ambivalence. Radegunde was herself a victim of violent and coercive power; her entire life was caught up in the various familial and dynastic struggles for power that surged around her, threatening every goal she pursued. It is not hard to understand how she might wish to renounce such power. But Radegunde seems to believe that destructive power is only put to flight by alternative power, a divine power that is mediated through persons who work and struggle in accord with grace and wisdom. She tried to exercise such power herself, forming her community and bringing her powers of persuasion to bear on her kin and associates. In the use of that power, she was both gentle and firm. But she also wanted to bring divine and just power into her world through mediators more efficacious than herself. To that end, she collected her relics not gently, but fiercely, not just through persuasion and example but by marshalling the forces of kings and their envoys. Radegunde was not, I think, ambivalent about power as such, but her experience had taught her the viciousness of coercive power and the dangerous hold which power can acquire over those who would wield it.

The Cross: Power and the Paradox of the Gospel

By the time of Radegunde's foundation at Poitiers, the cross of Christ had emerged as an object of devotion but had also, to some degree, been co-opted by the politically powerful. Although Christians followed the practice of making the sign of the cross with the hand before significant action and especially in marking the new Christian in baptism, there is little archeological evidence for the use of the cross as a Christian icon before the late fourth century. This is understandable as long as the cross remained an instrument of capital punishment. Early in the second century, Christian writers had begun to give typological interpretations of the cross, seeing in it a parallel with the Tree of Life in Paradise, the staff of Moses, and the bronze serpent made into a standard that healed the Israelites while they were in the desert (Numbers 21). For Eastern Christians who celebrated Easter according to the Johannine rather than the Synoptic chronology, the cross was the symbol of the triumph of life and light over death and darkness, but when the Roman custom of dating Easter became universal that symbolism gave way to the theological ideas of soteriological reconciliation and the salutary acceptance of suffering.

The beginnings of iconic use of the cross associated with Constantine's reign tied the symbolism of the cross once again to the notion of triumph, less a reminder of the Lord's crucifixion than of his Second Coming in glory. Early Christian accounts of Constantine's experiences at the battle of Milvian Bridge described a vision of a cross in the sky as the sign under which he would conquer and since his toleration of Christians seems to have begun with that event, the story and the symbol became emblematic both of military supremacy for Christian rulers and the liberation of the Church from its persecutors. The story is echoed in Gregory of Tours' account of Clovis' conversion, although Gregory does not explicitly use an image of the cross. However, Clovis seems to have considered himself "a new Constantine" and to have imitated the first Constantine in significant ways.[44] Certainly Gregory makes clear that Clovis is converted because he finds in the Christian God a source of military strength and the power to be victorious. It is clear that in the Kingdom of the Franks, the theology of the cross was a theology of triumph and even of conquest.[45]

We find that theology represented by a hymn written specifically for the translation of the relic of the cross to Poitiers, the "Vexilla Regis"[46] of Venantius Fortunatus, a formative figure in the literary circle from which

[44] See Richard Fletcher, *The Barbarian Conversion: From Paganism to Christianity* (Berkeley and Los Angeles: University of California Press, 1999) 106.

[45] Such a theology remained current, perhaps dominant, for many centuries. The cross on Crusaders' pennants and the regalia of the conquistadors are later, tragic reminders of the force of this interpretation of the cross.

[46] This hymn is still used in the Liturgy of the Eucharist and of the Hours but the present version omits Fortunatus' original vv. 2, 7, and 8 and adds two final verses not by Fortunatus. The translation used here is by Walter Kirkham Blount (d. 1717). See *home.earthlink.net/~thesaurus/thesaurus/Hymni/Vexilla.html*.

Baudonivia's life also comes. In his hymn, Fortunatus does note the redemptive character of Christ's death upon the cross; in the very first verse he plays on the mystery of life and death and the paradox that Christ's death restored life to all: "upon it Life did death endure,/ and yet by death did life procure."[47] He interprets the Johannine detail of the water and blood that pours from the pierced side of Christ as an act of cleansing for human defilement: "to wash us clear from stain of sin, pour out a flood/ of precious water mixed with blood."[48] He also interprets the death of Christ as a sacrifice: "here is the victim offered up by the powerful grace of redemption."[49] Yet the language and imagery—the sub-text, if you will—are redolent with triumph, royalty, and conquest. The cross is held high on banners (associated with military and royal processions)[50] and the blood associated with the crucifixion becomes a dye for royal garments. "O lovely and refulgent Tree,/ adorned with purpled majesty."[51] God rules the nations from a tree and all applaud the noble victory.[52]

One might assume from the way she tells the story of the translation of the relic of the cross to Poitiers that Baudonivia shares that theology. But there is significant evidence within the text, I believe, that she espouses, rather, a theology of the cross based on the Marcan Gospel and attributes the same theology to Radegunde.[53] For Mark, all of Christian discipleship is to be expressed as a sharing in the cross of

---

[47] "Qua vita mortem pertulit, et morte vitam protulit."

[48] "Ut nos lavaret sordibus, Manavit unda et sanguine."

[49] "redemptionis gratia/ hic immolata est hostia." From stanza 2 of Fortunatus' hymn, which was later omitted from the liturgical version. Trans. Dr. William Fulco, S.J., NEH professor of classics and archeology at Loyola Marymount University.

[50] "Vexilla Regis prodeunt, fulget Crucis mysterium."

[51] "Arbor decora et fulgida,/ ornate Regis purpura." Stanza 5.

[52] "Regnavit a ligno Deus," Stanza 4 and "plaudis triumpho nobili" from Stanza 7. Stanza 7 was also omitted from the later liturgical version and has been translated by Dr. William Fulco, S.J.

[53] Schulenburg notes the complex set of motivations behind medieval women saints' self-imposed suffering, including the desire to imitate Christ in his sufferings. She acknowledges the validity of the spiritual motivation as well as its dangerous possibilities for obsessive, self-hating behavior. She does not, however, connect the commitment to the cross to the theme of service, a connection I believe present in the Baudonivia *vita*.

Christ and as service to others. Exegetes have long commented on the dominance of the Passion in Mark's Gospel; some have called the Gospel "a passion narrative with an introduction." At the very heart of Mark, chs. 8:22–10:52, is a carefully constructed narrative built around three predictions of the passion that become opportunities for Christ to explain discipleship. This central section begins and ends with a miracle story of the healing of a blind man. The first healing, before the predictions of the passion begin, is a strange story indeed. The man is unnamed, brought to Jesus by others, and Jesus has difficulty with the healing; he must lay his hand on the blind man twice before his sight is completely restored. In the story that concludes the section under consideration, the blind man is named and aggressively seeks healing, "shouting," "jumping," and running to Jesus in spite of his blindness and in spite of the displeasure of the crowd. He is immediately healed by a single word from Jesus. Most exegetes see these two miracles as statements about the faith of the disciples and their ability to grasp the teaching of Jesus. The teaching that is given between the two miracles enables the disciples to begin to believe. It is the teaching on discipleship.

Each of the four Gospels locates Jesus' teaching on discipleship differently. In Matthew, it comes in the form of the five discourses, especially in the Sermon on the Mount, introduced by the Beatitudes. Luke has Jesus teach his followers the meaning of discipleship on the long journey from Galilee to Jerusalem, en route to Calvary whence "he will be taken up into heaven" (Luke 9:51). In John, the teaching comes within the intimacy and drama of the Last Supper Discourse. For Mark, however, the teaching on discipleship is placed between the two miracles of sight and is directly appended to the three predictions of the passion. After the first prediction, Mark's Jesus says that the disciple "must renounce self; he must take up his cross and follow me" (8:34). He reinforces this teaching by the paradox saying about saving one's life by losing it "for my sake and the sake of the gospel" (v. 35). In these verses, the cross is not a symbol or a metaphor, but represents the real, physical suffering the disciple must undergo; exegetes agree that Mark's audience faced Roman persecution and the real possibility of death. After the second prediction, the teaching is subtly changed and enlarged. There discipleship is identified with service: "If anyone wants to be first, he must make himself last of all and servant of all" and must receive and care for children—symbolic of the vulnerable—as for Christ himself (9:35-37). After the third prediction, discipleship is again identified with service and Mark concludes this teaching on discipleship by having Jesus give the ultimate motivation for it. "For the Son of Man did not come to be served but to serve, and to give his life as a ransom for many" (10:43-45).

The disciples in Mark's narrative show by word and behavior that they consider these mandates difficult, too difficult in fact for them, since Mark records that they all desert him rather than take up their own crosses and follow. On Calvary, only the women remain and Mark notes that they had "looked after him when he was in Galilee" (15:40-41), that is, they had served him in life and followed him all the way to the cross. They are, therefore, in Mark's own terms, the true disciples of Jesus.

Although Baudonivia does not faithfully reproduce the structure and themes of Mark's Gospel, there are sufficient echoes within her text to suggest that she has adopted his theology of the cross. There are, first of all, two miracles of sight restored to those who petition Radegunde, a matron named Mammezo who prays in her oratory near Saix and a Bishop Leo who prays while in contact with her hair shirt. Baudonivia's stories do not frame material that is in any way reflective of Mark's, but the first, along with the miracle of Vinoberga, introduces Radegunde's collection of relics and the bishop's healing introduces her efforts to obtain the relic of the cross. As faith stories they suggest that it is through faith alone that relics can be appreciated and their benefit reaped. Indeed, immediately after the healing of Bishop Leo and as Baudonivia begins to speak of the relic of the cross, she comments that Radegunde would happily "have petitioned the Lord Himself . . . to dwell here in sight of all. But what she could not see with her carnal eyes, she could contemplate with her spiritual mind sedulously intent on prayer."[54] It is a comment about faith, the divine presence and the value of visible reminders of that presence.

Her efforts to obtain relics express her desire to have visible signs of the presence of the saints to stimulate the faith of the people and to give them access to the saints' power. In seeking the relic of the cross,

---

[54] "Post congregatas sanctorum reliquias, si fieri potuisset, ipsum Dominum de sede majestatis suae visibiliter hic habitare expetisset. Quamquam eum carnalis oculus non intueretur, spiritalis mens intenta sedulis precibus contemplabatur." Krusch 387, l. 33–35.

Radegunde wants to bring to Poitiers a visible reminder of Christ's presence, to enable the faithful to see by faith what Radegunde herself already knows by faith, that the power of the cross is with them and exactly what the power of the cross is. In a world full of different kinds of power, the power of the cross must be proclaimed to the people. The interplay of faith and sight, suggested by the two miracles in Baudonivia's text and made explicit in her comment that links the healing of the bishop to the story of the relic of the cross, make these two miracles echoes of the sight miracles in Mark's Gospel and, like his miracles, connected to discipleship of the crucified Christ. Even more strongly, however, does Baudonivia play on the Marcan themes of discipleship in her description of Radegunde's service within the monastery at Poitiers and beyond it. She develops her theology of service in a long and complex chapter (#8) in which she describes Radegunde's service, talks about her relationship to the sisters at Holy Cross Monastery and speaks of Radegunde's relationship to those who persecute her.

Feminist historians and critics have noted what they call a "domestication" of female sanctity in the written lives of early medieval women saints. Jo Ann McNamara persuasively documents the way in which the Theodosian empresses and Merovingian queens imitated the life of St. Helena, as documented by Socrates and Eusebius. According to McNamara, Helena sets the example by transforming "the power she derived from Constantine into a 'womanly' model of Christian monarchy connected to piety, charity and mercy, royal qualities hard to reconcile with the warlike and coercive aspect of masculine rule."[55] Later queens and empresses imitated Helena in building churches and monasteries, working as peacemakers, bestowing charitable largesse and promoting the cult of relics. McNamara finds the connections between Radegunde and Helena particularly strong, largely because of their shared devotion to the relic of the cross. All these royal women, according to McNamara, occupy a "perilous position between powerful husbands and powerless people [that] may have fitted them peculiarly well to share the uniqueness of royal power and exercise it in certain unwarlike activities, which could be characterized as 'woman's work.'"[56]

---

[55] Jo Ann McNamara, "Imitatio Helenae," 52–53.

[56] Ibid., 63.

The historian Suzanne Wemple reads Baudonivia's text as introducing new elements into the conventional presentation of saintly women by presenting Radegunde as a peacemaker and leader of a cult center. Yet she too thinks that Radegunde's service to pilgrims and the sick reflects an attempt to domesticate her power and affirms that Baudonivia shows "the assimilation into religious life of the nurturing and mediatory roles women were expected to play as daughters and wives in Merovingian society.[57]

This point of view lives on, if with some nuance. More recently Lynda Coon has espoused the position that in the life written by Fortunatus, Radegunde has been fitted into the mold "of a Merovingian Elijah, Samuel and Christ," a theme deliberately tamed by the portrait of her as servant. The "bishop's Radegund on the whole resembles the charitable, domestic women servants in the New Testament and more closely fits the model of a Merovingian Martha than that of a great prophet."[58] These critical judgments, like those about asceticism in women's texts discussed above, are significant and, in general, borne out by the primary sources. But Coon is right to specify that this is Fortunatus' interpretation and her reference to the women in the New Testament is suggestive, if dismissive. The Gospels offer different interpretations of the service of women, as do the hagiographical texts. Fortunatus names Radegunde a "Martha," an early reference to that biblical woman who, together with her sister Mary, symbolized the dichotomy of behaviors expected of Christians—contemplation and charitable service.[59]

Baudonivia makes a veiled reference to this line of interpretation when she says that Radegunde had so committed herself to ascetical practice "that she easily deserved to devote herself to God alone" (8), a reference to contemplation focused entirely on God. However, Baudonivia contradicts the notion that service is a tamer, domesticated choice. She says that when Radegunde served pilgrims and the sick she had fortified

[57] Wemple, *Women in Frankish Society*, 183.

[58] Lynda L. Coon, *Sacred Fictions: Holy Women and Hagiography in Late Antiquity* (Philadelphia: University of Pennsylvania Press, 1997) 127.

[59] For the interpretation of the biblical sisters Martha and Mary during the Middle Ages, see Giles Constable, *Three Studies in Medieval Religious and Social Thought* (Cambridge: The University of Cambridge Press, 1995) 1–141.

herself with even stronger arms (a military reference). "Then, however, dressed with stronger arms, without ceasing in the prayers, the vigils and the important reading [that she did], she herself served food to pilgrims at table, and she herself with her own hands washed and cleaned the feet of the sick."[60] The work of service is a more demanding task; it requires greater fortification through prayer, the keeping of vigils and the reading of Scripture. The use of military language seems to contravene the notion that personal service is a domestic chore and Baudonivia says that Radegunde chose service as the more difficult and meritorious task. Baudonivia's complete development of Radegunde's commitment to service bears out this alternative view.

She says of Radegunde that "she did not permit a servant to give comfort to her, because she, in her devotion, ran about to fulfill service."[61] Baudonivia specifies that Radegunde served food to travelers and washed the feet of the sick with her own hands. This is a clear echo of Mark's description of Jesus as the servant whom true disciples are to imitate: "The Son of Man did not come to be served but to serve" (10:43). It also echoes, of course, the Last Supper narrative where Jesus demonstrates what the service of the disciples ought to be by washing their feet. Like the Last Supper, also, Radegunde's service flourishes within the context of a loving community of believers. Radegunde so loves her flock that "she no longer remembered that she had a family and a royal husband;" she tells her sisters that she has chosen them and she invites them to work with her, to serve the Lord "in this world so that [they] may rejoice together in the world to come."[62]

---

[60] "Quo tamen tempore fortioribus armis induta, sine cessatione orationibus, vigiliis, lectione propensa, peregrinis ipsa cibos ministravit ad mensam, ipsa suis manibus lavit et tersit infirmantum vestigia." Krusch 382, ll. 33 p. 383, l. 2. (Crawford trans.)

[61] "Non famulae permisit sibi dare solatium, quod devota concursitabat inplere servitium . . . ." Ibid., 383, ll. 2–3. (Crawford trans.)

[62] "Congregationem, quam in nomine Domini plena Dei desiderio congregavit, in tantumque dilexit, ut etiam parentes vel regem coniugum se habuisse nec reminisceretur. Quod frequenter nobis dum praedicaret, dicebat: 'Vos elegi filias, vos mea lumina, vos, mea vita, vos, mea requies totaque felicitas, vos, novella plantatio. Agite mecum in hoc saeculo, unde gaudeamus in futuro. Plena fide plenoque cordis affectu serviamus Domino,' . . ." Krusch 383, ll. 21–26.

Again this theme is a recasting of what is found in the Marcan Gospel. At the end of chapter 3, Jesus' family come to see him and his response is the rhetorical declamation "Who are my mother and my brothers? Whoever does the will of God is my brother and sister and mother" (3:33-34). As Mark's Jesus bids his disciples, Radegunde has "forgotten" her royal family and chosen a family of those invited to do God's will with her, to work with her in the world, to serve as she does. This is matter of generosity and of joy. To her sisters, Baudonivia says, Radegunde offered "undiluted wine," a phrase that has biblical resonance suggesting wisdom, joy, and the vitality of life itself. Baudonivia draws together the themes of service, specifically table service and foot-washing, and of voluntary community, a community assembled in the name of God's love. She speaks of the way in which the bonds of love between disciples replaces the bonds of blood kinship and of the joy and vitality that flow within and outward from a community of discipleship. Finally, also in chapter 8, Baudonivia describes Radegunde's control over her speech, "never uttering slander or lies or curses." She then says that the saintly queen "always prays for her persecutors and taught others to do the same." This too is an echo of a gospel injunction, not from Mark this time but from Matthew's Sermon on the Mount (5:34), the section in which Matthew develops his theology of discipleship. All of this reflects the gospel traditions about discipleship with a particular emphasis on Mark's teaching that discipleship is in relationship to the cross.

Two final passages in the text further associate her with a theology of the cross. The first comes in chapter 11 as Baudonivia tells the story of Mammezo's plea for healing. Baudonivia says that Radegunde "who took everyone's sorrow upon herself alone, as long as she lived, responded kindly to the invocation of her name."[63] The allusion here is to the Suffering Servant in Isaiah, whose four songs were woven into the liturgy of Passiontide and Holy Week, with specific reference to the sufferings of Christ. "We despised him, we held him of no account, an object from which people turn away their eyes. Yet it was our afflictions he

---

[63] "Sic illa, quae dolores omnium in se sola transtulit, dum in corpore fuit, usque dum eas mederi potuisset, benigne exaudivit ad invocationem nominis sui." Ibid., 385, ll. 23–25.

was bearing, our pain he endured . . ." (Isa 53:3-4). Like Christ the Suffering Servant, Radegunde bears the sorrows of others, mourning with those who mourn. The second passage is found in chapter 18 in which Baudonivia describes Radegunde thus: "wherever she went she followed the Lord in spirit imitating the teacher of humility who descended to earth from his heavenly throne."[64] The allusion here is to the so-called kenosis hymn of Philippians 2, a text also associated with liturgical celebrations of the Lord's passion and death. The Lord who was with God did not cling to his position at God's right hand but emptied himself to become a servant, taking that service all the way to death. So Baudonivia describes Radegunde the queen who did not cling to royal position and privileges but became the servant of all and served unto the day of her death.

One may continue to see the effects of a gender-driven attempt to domesticate women's power in Baudonivia's insistence on Radegunde's service. But read theologically, the text speaks also of Christian discipleship as it is very specifically laid out in the Gospels, particularly the Gospel of Mark. Evangelical discipleship requires the voluntary acceptance of the cross and its profound connection with a life of Christian service. Radegunde the saintly queen, whose secular and spiritual power are well demonstrated in Baudonivia's text, works tirelessly to bring a relic of the holy cross to the city of Poitiers; all her biographers portray this event as the apex of her public benefaction and of her personal power and holiness. It is not surprising therefore to find in Baudonivia's portrait a carefully drawn image of one who is a true disciple of the crucified Lord as prescribed by Mark's Gospel. The cross as relic is the touchstone of Radegunde's public life; devotion to the cross of Christ through suffering and service is the touchstone of her spiritual life and identity. Freely does Radegunde accept the sufferings that come to her, taking up her cross to follow Jesus; even more freely does she minister, in Christ's name, to the poor and the sick. She who was first in the house by reason of her royal identity and her function as foundress became the last and the servant of all.

---

[64] "Tantum denique donum in se, largiente divina gratia, habuit, ut humilitatis magistrum, qui de caeli solio ad terras descendit, imitando Dominum in spiritu sequeretur, cocumque ierit." Ibid., 390, ll. 19–21.

This understanding of service, as the appropriate response to the divine initiative of salvation wrought through a crucified Savior, brings Baudonivia's text into the center of a theological conversation about the meaning of Christ's redemptive death. Indeed, a Marcan understanding of service would seem to be the hermeneutic key, not only to the life of Radegunde, but also to the New Testament understanding of the cross as well. In his monumental study *Jesus: An Experiment in Christology*, Edward Schillebeeckx has made a careful historical critical study of the New Testament textual evidence about the interpretation of the death of Christ. He notes that although there is only slight evidence in the oldest level of gospel material for a soteriological interpretation of Christ's death, "in Mark 10:45 a clear connection is made between the theme of *diakonein* or service on Jesus' part and that of an expiatory death: 'For the son of man also came not to be served but to serve, and to give his life as a ransom for many.'"[65] Schillebeeckx describes how the secular Greek meaning of the word of *diakonein*—waiting at table—was transformed into a specifically Christian and ecclesial notion of service and he attributes the shift in meaning to something that happened at the Last Supper to lead Christ's followers to an understanding of the meaning of his whole mission. He concludes that "the notion of *diakonia*, service(-ability), is the reflection of a very early interpretation of Jesus' death, anchored in the Last Supper tradition."[66] He further notes that in the Lucan variant (22:27), this logion becomes a teaching with both ecclesial and ethical implications that are made clear in liturgical usage.

According to Schillebeeckx, the existence of this early tradition lays the groundwork for a soteriological interpretation of the washing of the feet in John's Last Supper Discourse, and he sees in both the related Johannine and Lucan passages a further connection made between the service of Jesus, the ritual meal and the Parousia of Jesus. "Serving, service performed out of love, thus becomes the final stamp set upon the life of Jesus; it is carried over from a historical event to the Lord who is to come."[67] Schillebeeckx notes the many examples in Jesus' historical life

---

[65] Edward Schillebeeckx, *Jesus: An Experiment in Christology*, trans. Hubert Hoskins (New York: The Seabury Press, 1979) 303.

[66] Ibid., 304.

[67] Ibid., 305.

when the offer of God's salvation is set within the context of a meal, specifically his table-fellowship with sinners and the miraculous feedings of the multitudes.

Finally, Schillebeeckx reads the Marcan version of the "words of institution" as indicating both a conviction of his own death and assurance of a larger hope. His death was for him the final rejection by those he had come to serve and to save, a failure of the highest order; yet it did not obviate his conviction that God's plan for salvation would not be frustrated. "An experience of a historical failure and at the same time a passionate faith in God's future for man [sic] is for the religious person no contradiction, but a mystery eluding every attempt at theoretical or rational accommodation."[68]

In Schillebeeckx's analysis, the understanding of Jesus as Servant, and his death as the ultimate service, provides the oldest Christian understanding of the Christ's crucifixion as a soteriological reality, a death on behalf of others. This theological perspective comes from a reflection on Jesus' behavior at the Last Supper, in which he acts as host, washes the feet of the disciples, offers a cup of wine that he understands to be his last, but not without hope. The germ of this theology of the cross would, in Schillebeeckx's judgment, go back to the person of Jesus himself.

Similarly, Walter Kasper in *Jesus the Christ*[69] holds that the gospel idea of Jesus as servant is the hermeneutic key to grasping Christ's own self-understanding. He shows how Jesus embodied the Kingdom of God that he proclaimed in repeated service to others and this service demonstrates the liberation that marks God's kingdom. For him, Christ's service establishes a new community among his followers and between them and God, thus removing human alienation and suffering at its roots. To live, then, a life of similar service, loving even one's enemies is truly to be a follower of Christ. Kasper believes that his mode of life would inevitably have brought Jesus to understand his death also as a service for others and therefore as a sacrifice. "In other words," Kasper concludes, "he saw his death as a representative and saving service to

[68] Ibid., 310.
[69] Walter Kasper, *Jesus the Christ*, trans. V. Green (New York: Paulist Press, 1976).

many."[70] Therefore, in Kasper's thought, living a life of service brought Jesus to understand the theological meaning of his own life and, in parallel fashion, reflecting on Jesus as Servant brought Christians to understand the theological and soteriological significance of Christ's death. To imitate that life of service is not only to be a true disciple, it is the path to theological understanding as well.

Jesus, then, came to understand his own mission, and the death that fulfilled it, by serving others—his own disciples and the dispossessed especially—in a direct and material way. In Baudonivia's text, Radegunde follows Christ's example in serving others—her own sisters and the dispossessed pilgrims and sick—and so, we may conclude, comes to understand the cross whose relic she has obtained, as Christ did, not as the image on banners of conquest but as the sign of redemption beyond worldly power. Radegunde perceives the essential and intimate connection between service, especially the service of table fellowship, the washing of the feet and Christ's gift of self on the cross.

Like Schillebeeckx, Baudonivia draws the connection between the miraculous feedings and God's offer of salvation, as it takes place in Radegunde's life. When the queen is given a single cask of wine to dispense as she will, it never runs dry, no matter how often she draws from it. "The Lord fed five thousand men with five loaves and two fishes," says Baudonivia, "and His servant, whenever she saw poverty, refreshed people from this small amount for a whole year" (1). She shows us a Radegunde who chooses to serve rather than to be served and who, specifically, waits on pilgrims at table and washes the feet of the weak. She depicts the connection between a life of Christian discipleship through service and the formation of a community of believers that takes the place of a blood family. She portrays a Radegunde who empties herself progressively as the narrative continues, leaving her royal position, divesting herself of jewels and riches, espousing ever more severe fasts and penances until she had completed the race she had begun. Baudonivia describes her death as the culmination of "a long martyrdom for the love of the Lord," (21)[71] thus reinforcing Radegunde's imitation of Christ crucified in her own death. Service, her own life of

---

[70] Ibid., 120.
[71] Crawford trans.

serving others, has taught her, as it taught Jesus himself, the theological meaning of the cross and the power for salvation that is to be found in the total gift of self, voluntarily surrendered. In this context, the description of Radegunde's service is not merely a domestication of queenly power—though it may have been influenced by that trend of royal hagiography as well—but an integral and hermeneutic step toward the comprehension of the meaning of the cross. This was a source of the power symbolized by the icon of the cross.

Conclusion

The cross as a symbol of, and a mandate for, the inversion of the exercise of human power had been present in the Christian tradition from the earliest days. It is there in the Pauline literature, most especially the correspondence to the Corinthian community fractured by allegiance to apostles based on their natural gifts, a jockeying for eminence among the factions, a search for the more ostentatious gifts of the Spirit, and a scandalous division between the rich and the poor. To them Paul offers his most impassioned critique and a theology of human power. He affirms that the crucified Christ is the basis of their unity, that the Eucharist that celebrates and effects Christian unity is the playing out of Christ's gift of self on the cross (ch. 11). He sets up a powerful and uncompromising antithesis between the wisdom of God, which is revealed in the folly of the Cross, and the power of God, which is revealed in the weakness of the crucified Christ and of those who are his apostles (ch. 1). God's choice of the weak of the world to confound the strong gives theological and practical shape to Paul's ministry. He tells the story of his own folly and weakness, through which the powerful grace of God is revealed (2 Cor 11–12).

Throughout 1 Corinthians, he speaks repeatedly of himself and other apostles as servants, even slaves, who are already condemned to death as was the one they serve. He has even chosen to work with his own hands, that he might the more fully imitate Christ the servant and take his place among the poor whom Christ has chosen to honor. For Paul this is not an ascetical choice, but a soteriological imperative. He lives according to "the folly of the Cross" in order to share in its blessings and to confer those blessings upon others, in order that the redemption of Christ may be proclaimed and received. He imitates the crucified Christ because he reveals the God who sends him and the love and power of that redeeming God. That is what makes the practice of Christian love "the most excellent gift" (1 Cor 13). It is in the light of the Pauline theology of power that we must read Baudonivia's life of St. Radegunde. She tells of the struggle between the power of God and political power. She narrates Radegunde's use of power—both worldly and spiritual—on behalf of those who are without power and she proposes service as the means to live the reality of the cross in one's own life. She makes clear that to do so is to live at the heart of the redemptive mystery.

In the theological world that Radegunde and Baudonivia inhabit, there were few resources, beyond the Scriptures themselves, for reflecting upon a theology of power. In spite of the firm foundation laid down by St. Paul, there was little theological reflection on the relationship of worldly power to the power of the cross. Especially after Constantine, the cross as icon came to represent the wedding of Christian faith to political dominance and in the Merovingian Christian kingdom, sheer brute force and the power of military might, wealth, and aristocratic identity prevailed. Gregory of Tours regrets the excess of violence but sees a divine providence at work within it. In his hymn "Vexilla Regis," Fortunatus speaks of Christ's death on the cross, but he borrows all the symbolism of regalia to do so. He thereby makes worldly power the analogy for the power of the cross rather than, as Paul had done, using the power of the cross to critique its worldly counterpart. Both Gregory and Fortunatus see in Radegunde a victim of that power who, nonetheless, survives it to become holy. Baudonivia, on the other hand, does not tell the early stories of Radegunde's capture and enforced marriage; she does not show Radegunde as a victim but as one who searches for her place in the redemptive plan, the place where she may understand and use her power in the service of salvation. In her text we first see Radegunde as a saintly queen using her royal power to effect good ends: the redemption of captives, contributions to the needy and the destruction of pagan places of worship. She is using her power according to the models all around her, power as practiced by princes and bishops, with a recourse to coercive means, but for worthy ends.

Then she separates herself from the position of her power and moves, in gradual steps, toward the monastery of the Holy Cross. As a pilgrim, she is searching for her place in the world where people's lives are structured according to their power. In her search, she explores the ways of spiritual power, again using the models that are present in her world. She consults prophetic holy men, enlists those holy by profession, the bishops, and seeks relics. To some degree, she has renounced human power; but she continues to use the resources of the world in the service of others. She engages in political peacemaking and, most of all, creates a safe refuge and a place of opportunity for women of all classes in the convent of the holy cross. She seems to understand the ambiguity of using worldly power for spiritual ends but whenever she has recourse to such power, she attempts to subvert it through the practice of asceticism.

Finally, her struggles on behalf of others, and especially her pursuit of the most significant relic of all, that of the cross, seems to bring her to an awareness of the paradox of the power of God. When Baudonivia narrates the important center of her life, her life in the monastery of the Holy Cross, she emphasizes the way in which the Queen has patterned her life after the discipleship proclaimed by the Gospel of Mark. Putting herself aside, she serves others with her own hands, imitating not only Martha who welcomed Christ into her home, but the women in the gospel who left their homes, as Radegunde had done, to follow Jesus, ministered to him and stood in fidelity at the foot of the cross. She emptied herself and became a servant to all. She chose as family, not those to whom she was united by blood and were the source of her worldly power, but those who had gathered in the love of God. She makes an evangelical choice to act on behalf of women, who have little or no power to act on their own behalf. She mourns with those who mourn and suffers the persecution of those who would deny her the true cross so that she might bring about some justice, for the women of Holy Cross and for the people of Poitiers. Like Jesus himself, Radegunde learns the meaning of redemption and the power of the cross by serving those whom God loves. "Son though he was, he learned obedience through suffering," and she, his beloved disciple, learned the meaning of who he truly was by serving those who were the least of all.

It is extremely important to note that, in accordance with Jesus' injunction as Mark gives it, Radegunde chooses, not suffering, but service. To choose suffering is dangerous for all Christians, men and women alike. It may be even more dangerous for Christian women if, like asceticism, it is chosen out of an erroneous conviction that suffering, in itself, is pleasing to God or if it comes from a hatred of the body. To choose service is not a dangerous choice for any Christian. Genuine Christian service is not an act of self-denigration, though it is an act of genuine humility, made in full recognition of one's dignity and gifts. In a world in which coercive power is honored, the choice to serve can be perceived as weakness and mere docility. It may be thought a choice that sets a Christian outside the pale where influence may be exerted for the good. But for the Christian who is deeply committed to Christ, the Lord who came not to be served but to serve, it is a choice that gives access to the power of the Redeemer, to the God to whom all things are possible and who exercises power through the Cross. This is the theology that Baudonivia proposes in her life of St. Radegunde. When women came to the theological conversation from their usual place on the margins of the community, they brought a lived insight into the redemptive character of the cross.

Bibliography

Primary Sources

Ælred. "Genealogia regum anglorum." *PL* 195, cols. 711D–738A.

Anglo-Saxon Chronicle, The. Trans. and ed. M. J. Swanton. New York : Routledge, 1998.

Anselm. *On the Virgin Conception and Original Sin.* Trans. Camilla McNab. In *Anselm Of Canterbury: The Major Works.* Ed. Brian Davies and G. R. Evans. Oxford: Oxford University Press, 1998.

Augustine. "Sermo 347," *PL* 139, cols. 1524f. English trans. is *The Lord's Sermon on the Mount. Ancient Christian Writers* 5. Trans. John J. Jepson. Westminster, Md.: Newman Press, 1956.

Baudonivia. *De vita sanctae Radegundis, Liber II.* Ed. Krusch. *MGH SRM* 2:377–95.

Bede. *Ecclesiastical History of the English Church and Peoples.* Trans. Leo Sherley-Price. London: Penguin Books, 1955.

Boniface. *The Letters of Saint Boniface,* Trans. Ephraim Emerton. New York: Columbia University Press, 1940.

Dhuoda, *Manual pour mon fils.* Ed. Pierre Riché. Trans. Bernard de Vrégille and Claude Mondésert. *SC* 225. Paris: Editions du Cerf, 1975. The English trans. is Carol Neel, *Handbook for William: A Carolingian Woman's Counsel for Her Son.* Lincoln and London: University of Nebraska Press, 1991.

Eadmer. *A History of Recent Events in England.* Trans. G. Bosanquet. London: Cressit Press, 1964.

Gregory of Tours. *History of the Franks.* Trans. L. Thorpe. London: Penguin Books, 1974.

———. *The Glory of the Confessors.* Trans. Raymond Van Dam. Liverpool: Liverpool University Press, 1988.

———. *The Glory of the Martyrs.* Trans. Raymond Van Dam. Liverpool: Liverpool University Press, 1988.

Hildebert of Lavardin, *Vita radegundis. PL* 171, cols. 965A ff.

Irenaeus. *Against the Heresies. The Ante-Nicene Fathers.* Vol I. Ed. A. Roberts and J. Donaldson. Grand Rapids, Mich.: Wm. B. Eerdmans, 1979.

Jonas of Bobbio. *Vita sancti Columbani abbatis. PL* 87, 1013d-1014A.

Orderic Vitalis. *Ecclesiastical History.* 6 vols. Ed. and trans. Majorie Chibnall. Oxford: Clarendon Press, 1969–80.

Peter Lombard. *The Sentences,* in *A Scholastic Miscellany: Anselm to Ockham.* Ed. Eugene R. Fairweather. Philadelphia: Westminster Press, 1956.

Rudolf of Fulda. *B. Rabani Mauri Vita PL* 107, cols. 39–64.

———. *Vita Leobae Abbatissae Biscofesheimensis actore Rudolfo Fuldensi. MGH, SS* 15,1. Ed. G. Waitz, 118–31.

Tertullian. *The Flesh of Christ. The Ante-Nicene Fathers,* III. Ed. and trans. Alexander Roberts and James Donaldson. Grand Rapids, Mich.: Wm. B. Eerdmans, 1976.

Turgot. *Vita Margaritae. AASS* 19, 328–40.

Venantius Fortunatus. "De Virginitate," *Opera Poetica, MGH AA.* 4/1, 189–91.

———. *Vita sanctae Radegundis liber I.* Ed. Krusch. *MGH, SRM* 2:364–377.

———. "Vexilla Regis Prodeunt." Trans. Walter Kirkham Blount. home.earthlink.net/~thesaurus/thesaurus/Hymni/Vexilla.html.

William of Malmesbury. *Chronicle of the Kings of England.* Trans. J. A. Giles. London: George Bell and Sons, 1895.

Secondary Sources

Aigrain, René. *Sainte Radegonde.* Paris: Librairie Victor Lecoffre, 1918.

Alford, John A. "The Scriptural Self." In *The Bible in the Middle Ages: Its Influence on Literature and Art.* Ed. Bernard S. Levy. Binghamton, N.Y.: Medieval & Renaissance Texts & Studies, 1992.

Avray, D. L. "Peter Damian, Consanguinity and Church Property." In *Intellectual Life in the Middle Ages: Essays Presented to Margaret Gibson.* Ed. Lesley Smith and Benedicta Ward. London: Hambledon Press, 1992.

Bell, Rudolph. *Holy Anorexia.* Chicago and London: University of Chicago Press, 1985.

Brown, Peter. "The Rise and Function of the Holy Man in Late Antiquity." In *Society and the Holy in Late Antiquity.* Oxford and Los Angeles: University of California Press, 1982, 103–52.

———. *The Rise of Western Christendom.* Oxford: Blackwell Publications, 1996.

———. *The Cult of the Saints.* Chicago: The University of Chicago Press, 1981.

Bynum, Caroline. *Jesus As Mother.* Berkeley: University of California Press, 1982.

Chenu, Marie-Dominique. *Notes quotidiennes au Concile.* Ed. Alberto Mellone. Paris: Éditions du Cerf, 1995.

Chibnall, Margaret. *Anglo-Norman England 1066–1166.* Oxford: Basil Blackwell, 1986.

Congar, Yves. *L'Écclésiologie du Haut Moyen Âge*. Paris: Éditions du Cerf, 1968.

Constable, Giles. *Three Studies in Medieval Religious and Social Thought*. Cambridge: The University of Cambridge Press, 1995.

Coon, Lynda L. *Sacred Fictions: Holy Women and Hagiography in Late Antiquity*. Philadelphia: University of Pennsylvania Press, 1997.

Countryman, L. M. *The Rich Christian in the Church of the Early Empire: Contradictions and Accommodations*. New York and Toronto: Edwin Mellen Press, 1988.

Douglas, David C. and George W. Greenaway, eds. *English Historical Documents*. Vol. II: 1042–189. London and New York: Oxford University Press, 1981.

Evans, G. R. *Anselm and Talking About God*. Oxford: Clarendon Press, 1978.

Filleau, Jean. *La Preuve Historique des Litanies de la grande Reyne de France, Sainte Radegonde*. Poitiers: Abraham Mounin Imprimeur et Libraire, 1943.

Fletcher, Richard. *The Barbarian Conversion: From Paganism to Christianity*. Berkeley and Los Angeles: University of California Press, 1999.

Geary, Patrick J. *Furta Sacra: Thefts of Relics in the Central Middle Ages*. Princeton: University Press, 1978.

———. "Saints, Scholars and Society: The Elusive Goal." In *Saints: Studies in Hagiography*. Ed. Sandro Sticca. Binghamton, New York: Medieval & Renaissance Texts & Studies, 1996.

Greenaway, George. "Boniface As a Man of Letters." In *The Greatest Englishman: Essays on St. Boniface and the Church at Crediton*. Ed. Timothy Reuter. Exeter: Paternoster Press, 1980.

Harmeling, Deborah. "Tetta, 'Noble in Conduct,' and Thecla, 'Shining Like a Light in a Dark Place,'" in *Medieval Women Monastics*. Ed. Miriam Schmitt and Linda Kulzer. Collegeville: Liturgical Press, 1996.

Head, Pauline. "'Integritas' in Rudolph of Fulda's *Vita Leobae Abbatissae*." *Parergon* New Series 13, 1 (July, 1995).

Heffernan, Thomas. *Sacred Biography*. New York and Oxford: Oxford University Press, 1988.

Heilbrun, Carolyn. *Writing a Woman's Life*. New York: Ballantine Books, 1988.

Holdsworth, Christopher. "Boniface the Monk." In *The Greatest Englishman*. Ed. Reuter. Exeter: Paternoster Press, 1980.

Hollis, Stephanie. *Anglo-Saxon Women and the Church*. Woodbridge: Boydell Press, 1992.

Huneycutt, Lois. J. "Intercession and the High Medieval Queen: The Esther Topos." In *Power of the Weak: Studies on Medieval Women*. Ed. Jennifer Carpenter and Sally-Beth MacLean. Urbana and Chicago: University of Illinois Press, 1995, 126–46.

Johnson, Elizabeth. *Friends of God and Prophets*. Ottawa: Novalis, 1998.

Kasper, Walter. *Jesus the Christ*. Trans. V. Green. New York: Paulist Press, 1976.

LeClercq, Jean. *The Love of Learning and the Desire for God*. Trans. Catharine Misrahi. New York: Fordham University Press, 1967.

Levison, Wilhelm. *England and the Continent in the Eighth Century*. Oxford: Clarendon Press, 1946.

Macy, Gary. "The Ordination of Women in the Early Middle Ages." *TS* 61 (2000) 481–507.

Mayeski, Marie Anne. "Excluded by the Logic of Control: Women in Medieval Society and Scholastic Theology." In *Equal at the Creation*. Ed. Joseph Martos and Pierre Hegy Toronto: University of Toronto Press, 1998.

———. *Dhuoda: Ninth Century Mother and Theologian*. Scranton: University of Scranton Press, 1995.

———. "'Let Women Not Despair': Rabanus Maurus on Women as Prophets." *TS* 58, 2 (1997) 237–53.

McKitterick, Rosamund. *The Frankish Church under the Carolingians*. London and New York: Longmans Press, 1983.

McNamara, Jo Ann. "*Imitatio Helenae:* Sainthood as an Attribute of Queenship." In *Saints: Studies in Hagiography*. Ed. Sandro Sticca. Binghamton, N.Y.: Medieval & Renaissance Texts & Studies, 1996, 51–80.

———. "Living Sermons: Consecrated Women and the Conversion of Gaul." *Peaceweavers,* Ed. Lillian Thomas Shank and John A. Nichols. Kalamazoo, Mich.: Cistercian Publications, 1987, 19–37.

Mitros, Joseph A. "Patristic Views of Christ's Salvific Work." *Thought* 42, 166 (Autumn, 1967) 415–47.

Nelson, Janet L. "Queens as Jezebels: The Careers of Brunhild and Balthild in Merovingian History." In *Medieval Women*. Ed. Derek Baker. Oxford: Basil Blackwell, 1978.

O'Loughlin, Thomas. *Celtic Theology: Humanity, World and God in Early Irish Writings*. New York: Continuum, 2000.

Schillebeeckx, Edward. *Jesus: An Experiment in Christology*. Trans. Hubert Hoskins. New York: Seabury Press, 1979.

Tibbetts Schulenburg, Jane. *Forgetful of their Sex: Female Sanctity and Society, CA 500-1100*. Chicago and London: University of Chicago Press, 1998.

———. "Saints' Lives as a Source for the History of Women." In *Medieval Women and the Sources of Medieval History*. Ed. Joel T. Rosenthal. Athens and London: University of Georgia Press, 1990.

Wallace-Hadrill, J. M. *The Barbarian West 400-1000*. London: Basil Blackwell, 1985.

Ward, Benedicta. *Miracles and the Medieval Mind*. Philadelphia: University of Pennsylvania Press, 1987.

Wemple, Suzanne. *Women in Frankish Society: Marriage and the Cloister 500-900*. Philadelphia: University of Pennsylvania Press, 1988.

Wybourne, Catherine. "Leoba: A Study in Humanity and Holiness." In *Medieval Women Monastics*. Ed. Miriam Schmitt and Linda Kulzer. Collegeville: Liturgical Press, 1996.

Index

Adam, 28, 29, 32, 33, 34, 35, 36, 37, 38, 39, 41, 42, 44, 47, 48, 49, 50, 51, 52, 53, 54
almsgiving, 110, 111, 112, 115, 122
Ambrose, St., 8, 111
ancestors, 13, 16, 19, 20, 22, 23, 24, 25, 26, 27, 28, 29, 30, 31, 32, 34, 39, 40, 46, 48, 51, 52, 57, 105
Anglo-Saxon Chronicle, 14
Anselm Archbishop of Canterbury, St., 13, 14, 28, 30, 33, 34, 35, 36, 37, 38, 39, 40, 41, 47, 49, 51, 79
anthropology, 6, 8, 27, 31, 32, 59, 84, 90, 92, 97
apostle, 9, 10, 60, 65, 68, 99, 102, 103, 144
apostolic, 10, 60, 63, 68, 98, 102, 103, 107
apostolic See, 68
Aquinas, St. Thomas, 1, 37
asceticism, 6, 19, 22, 53, 95, 112, 113, 115, 116, 118, 119, 137, 144, 146
Athanasius, St., 6, 8, 88
Augustine of Canterbury, St., 53, 56
Augustine of Hippo, St., 6, 8, 27, 33, 34, 35, 37, 40, 41, 47, 53, 56, 79, 80, 90, 91, 119, 120, 123

authority, 18, 22, 23, 33, 57, 59, 63, 64, 65, 67, 68, 72, 80, 93, 99, 108, 109, 114, 116, 117, 123

Baudonivia, 105, 107, 108, 109, 110, 111, 112, 113, 114, 115, 116, 117, 118, 119, 120, 121, 122, 123, 124, 125, 126, 127, 128, 129, 130, 131, 133, 135, 136, 137, 138, 139, 140, 141, 143, 145, 146, 147
Bede, 4, 5, 7, 53, 55, 56, 58, 68, 75, 76, 129
Bell, Rudolf, 95
biological, 21, 23, 24, 31, 32, 33, 36, 37, 38, 39, 41, 44, 46, 47, 48, 50, 52
bishop, 6, 8, 41, 55, 58, 59, 60, 63, 64, 65, 66, 68, 71, 72, 73, 75, 90, 99, 107, 111, 113, 136, 137
Bonaventure, St., 1
Boniface, St., 56, 57, 59, 60, 61, 62, 63, 64, 65, 67, 68, 69, 70, 71, 72, 73, 76, 80, 89, 98, 99, 100, 101, 102, 103
Brown, Peter, 88, 89, 105, 126, 128
Bynum, Caroline, 95

canons and canonical, 73, 78, 94, 102
capax dei, 27, 31

153

suffering, 43, 45, 111, 132, 133, 134, 139, 140, 142, 146
Sulpicius Severus, 6

teacher, 57, 61, 73, 74, 80, 84, 89, 90, 94, 95, 101, 103, 140
temperance, 51, 91, 95
Tertullian, 6, 33, 41, 44, 45, 46, 52, 88
testimony, 41, 58, 62, 70, 96, 98
Tetta, 60, 61, 62, 76, 85, 86, 87, 92, 93, 96, 100
the beatitudes, 90, 91, 134
theological category, 13, 32, 47
theology, 1, 2, 4, 5, 6, 7, 8, 9, 10, 11, 13, 17, 19, 24, 26, 30, 32, 34, 35, 36, 39, 40, 44, 45, 46, 47, 52, 53, 54, 55, 57, 59, 61, 63, 70, 74, 77, 78, 79, 83, 88, 89, 97, 98, 104, 106, 108, 112, 132, 133, 135, 136, 139, 141, 142, 143, 144, 145, 147
theology, local, 4, 5, 57
theology, systematic, 2, 4, 5
Turgot, 17, 18, 19, 20, 21, 22, 23, 24, 50
typology, 131

Venantius Fortunatus, 8, 20, 33, 107, 111, 118, 119, 121, 129, 132, 133, 137, 145

Vexilla Regis, 107, 132, 133, 145
vigil, 115, 117, 118, 121, 125, 129, 138
    Easter Vigil, 82
virginity, 53, 96
virtue, 3, 13, 17, 18, 19, 20, 21, 22, 23, 24, 25, 26, 27, 28, 29, 30, 31, 32, 34, 39, 40, 47, 50, 51, 54, 61, 62, 69, 77, 81, 86, 87, 89, 90, 91, 94, 95, 96, 97, 100, 109, 110, 115, 117, 120, 126
vocation, 26, 59, 60, 61, 62, 63, 74, 89, 90, 94, 95, 96, 97, 98

Ward, Benedicta, 50, 79, 119, 128
wealth, 13, 15, 16, 19, 21, 22, 28, 29, 43, 47, 48, 49, 52, 62, 108, 111, 112, 113, 116, 117, 122, 125, 143, 145
Wemple, Suzanne, 33, 106, 112, 114, 121, 124, 137
will, the, 35, 38, 67, 139
William of Malmesbury, 14
Wills, Garry, 6
wisdom, 10, 26, 43, 51, 56, 66, 67, 71, 73, 90, 91, 92, 94, 96, 104, 122, 123, 124, 125, 131, 139, 144
Word of God, 19, 42, 50, 52, 100, 104, 123
Wybourne, Catherine, 85

Docal theology - 4

Anselm S I C 34

Margaret - conclusion for reward 51

Status of le da 90

Lectio 93 - 123